T0133074

Software Requirements

Other CRC/Auerbach Publications in Software Development, Software Engineering, and Project Management

AUERBACH PUBLICATIONS
www.auerbach-publications.com
To Order Call: 1-800-272-7737 • Fax: 1-800-374-3401
E-mail: orders@crcpress.com

Software Requirements

Encapsulation, Quality, and Reuse

Rick Lutowski

Auerbach Publications
Taylor & Francis Group

Boca Raton   London   New York   Singapore

Published in 2005 by
Auerbach Publications
Taylor & Francis Group
6000 Broken Sound Parkway NW, Suite 300
Boca Raton, FL 33487-2742

© 2005 by Taylor & Francis Group, LLC
Auerbach is an imprint of Taylor & Francis Group

No claim to original U.S. Government works
Printed in the United States of America on acid-free paper
10 9 8 7 6 5 4 3 2 1

International Standard Book Number-10: 0-8493-2848-9 (Hardcover)
International Standard Book Number-13: 978-0-8493-2848-0 (Hardcover)
Library of Congress Card Number 2005042100

Library of Congress Cataloging-in-Publication Data

Lutowski, Rick.
    Software requirements : encapsulation, quality, and reuse / Rick Lutowski.
      p. cm.
    Includes bibliographical references and index.
    ISBN 0-8493-2848-9 (alk. paper)
      1. Software engineering. I. Title.

QA76.758.L87 2005
005.1--dc22   2005042100

Taylor & Francis Group
is the Academic Division of T&F Informa plc.

Visit the Taylor & Francis Web site at
http://www.taylorandfrancis.com

and the Auerbach Publications Web site at
http://www.auerbach-publications.com

Contents

Appendices

Preface

About This Book

Most requirements books today provide general-purpose guidance such as "involve the customer" and "make the requirements testable," or document-specific techniques such as Use Cases. In spite of this breadth of coverage, several important topics are weakly, rarely, or never covered in requirements books. These topics include the effect of requirements on overall software quality (weakly covered), requirements reuse (rarely covered), and requirements encapsulation (never covered). As its title suggests, *Software Requirements: Encapsulation, Quality, and Reuse* strives to remedy these shortcomings.

This book is able to cover these additional topics because it focuses on the concepts and techniques of the Freedom approach to requirements. Freedom is a lightweight, customer-centric technical software development methodology originally developed for NASA's Space Station Freedom Program. Freedom strives to meet customer needs for functionality by specifying requirements in an innovative manner that permits *encapsulation* of requirements in code objects for later ease of change. Requirements encapsulation in turn enables requirements *reuse*. Customer needs for quality are addressed by continuous emphasis on quality drivers throughout the development process. Direct participation of the customer, or a knowledgeable customer representative, is essential to the Freedom requirements process.

Freedom's approach to requirements involves a change in perspective. Rather than viewing requirements as statements about the software, Freedom considers requirements to be part of the software, namely, its external interface. Freedom involves customers in requirements specification by enlisting their help to specify the external interface of the software that they will use. With the assistance of the developers, customers specify the software external interface in terms of stimulus–response pairs organized into cohesive sets called "stimulus sets." The stimulus sets are themselves organized hierarchically into a "functionality tree" that defines the architecture of the external interface. During design, developers use the external interface architecture as the upper level of the design architecture, thus ensuring architectural identity between requirements and design. Within this upper level of design, a requirements encapsulating "functionality module" is created for each stimulus set of the functionality tree, thus ensuring architectural identity between requirements and implementation. A change to any requirement (external interface stimulus–response pair) is consequently localized by the architecture to one functionality module. Architectural symmetry effectively achieves requirements encapsulation in code modules, making requirements change easier throughout the life of the software, and enables requirements reuse, easing future development.

It is suggested that readers of this book have some prior understanding of object-oriented (OO) concepts. An OO background is helpful in understanding the Freedom concept of requirements encapsulation, which is built upon the OO concept of information-hiding. Due to its importance, information-hiding is reviewed in Chapter 2, but prior exposure to OO can ease comprehension.

Coding proficiency is also helpful in getting the most out of this book. Coding may seem like an unnecessary prerequisite for a requirements process. However, creation of a user interface (UI) mockup is a necessary step in the process. A UI mockup is program code that implements the proposed look and feel of the UI. It is an effective vehicle for obtaining user confirmation of requirements correctness very early in the development cycle when change is least expensive. Also, an explanation of the structure of a UI mockup provides insight into the practical aspects of encapsulation of requirements in code objects. For these reasons, the book covers creation of UI mockups. Hence, prior exposure to coding in general, and UI development in particular, is helpful.

The preferred programming language for Freedom is an OO language such as Java. Hence, the code examples in the book are in Java. However, Freedom can be used with any programming language that supports data encapsulation. This includes non-OO languages such as C or Fortran when such languages are used carefully.[1]

This book uses terminology from original information-hiding theory, and from modern object-oriented languages such as Java. Both sources use different words to describe the same or similar concepts. For example, the terms "module" and "class" both refer to a unit of code. Generally speaking, "module" is a generic term for a unit of code, and "class" is a unit of code in an OO programming language such as Java. Clarification of such terminology is provided by the Glossary.

References

1. Lutowski, R.N. 1995. Object-oriented software development with traditional languages. *Fortran Forum* 14: 4 (December).

Acknowledgments

Many individuals are inevitably involved with the development of something as large as a full life-cycle software methodology such as Freedom. In chronological order, those who have contributed to Freedom (even if they were not aware of it) include the following.

- The original members of the Naval Research Laboratory's Software Cost Reduction (SCR) project, especially Dr. David Parnas and David Weiss. The SCR project codified the concept of information-hiding and helped to make it a mainstay of software development today. Even though most software practitioners are unaware of the SCR team and its accomplishments, all owe SCR a huge debt of gratitude. My gratitude is far more personal, for the seeds of Freedom were sown as a result of working under David Weiss at the Software Productivity Consortium (SPC). David taught his SPC team information-hiding the way it was intended to be. Thanks also go out to Dr. Parnas, whose e-mails answered many long-standing questions.
- The late Dr. Harlan Mills, whose advocacy of black box theory for software engineering provided the key to defining requirements in a manner that permitted their encapsulation. May his contributions and memory live forever.
- Tom Durek, assignee to the Software Productivity Consortium, for his concept of a Canonical Information Processing System Architecture. Tom's "Canonical IPSA" inspired Freedom's Canonical Design Architecture (although it was necessary to shorten the name for the benefit of mere software engineers).
- Ron Blakemore and Jeff Kantor, the members of the Space Station Freedom Project (SSFP) Standards and Methods team who helped

xv

develop the object-oriented requirements encapsulation methodology for use on SSFP. Their technical insight and perseverance helped make requirements encapsulation a practical reality.

- The Freedom Ship International (FSI) In-house Software Development Team (ISDT) consisting of Chris Jacoby, Shing Lin, Gang Qi, Neeraj Tulsian, and Travis Watkins, who peer reviewed, and helped refine and document, the SSFP methodology for use within FSI. It was they who encouraged the anonymous SSFP methodology be given a real name: hence "Freedom."
- James McGovern, who provided much needed encouragement and advice during my quest to find a publisher for a book on Freedom.
- John Wyzalek and the other forward-thinking staff of Auerbach Publications, who exhibit the rare and wonderful quality of publishing technically compelling work even if it is not from a high-profile source.
- Last but not least, my wife and angel, Barbara, who provided every means of support prior to and during the production of this book.

Progress is the result of individuals such as the above all pulling on the oars together. Without them, Freedom and this book would not exist. My deepest thanks to all of you!

Chapter 1

Overview

1.1 Why Freedom?

There are already a large number of software methodologies. Is it really necessary to publish yet another one?

Requirements specification is both the boon and the bane of software engineering. Requirements are the most important part of software development. In the words of Brooks, "The most important function that the software builder performs for the client is the iterative extraction and refinement of the product requirements."[1] On the other hand, requirements comprise the most difficult and risk-prone part of the process. Boehm's[2] list of the top ten risks resulting in software project failure, summarized in Table 1.1, shows that requirements shortfalls account for four of the top six risk factors:

- #3 Incorrect determination of required functionality
- #4 Implementing wrong user interfaces
- #5 Implementing unnecessary functionality ("gold plating")
- #6 Frequent changes to the requirements

The works of Brooks and Boehm, as well as others, make it clear that requirements specification is the most important aspect of software engineering, yet is also the part of the process most in need of improvement. Existing methodologies, even if adequate in the areas of design and implementation, fall seriously short in the crucial area of requirements. According to both Brooks and Boehm, an improved approach to requirements is urgently needed.

Table 1.1   Top Ten Software Risks

Software Risk
Personnel shortfalls
Unrealistic schedules and budgets
Developing wrong software functions
Developing wrong user interfaces
Gold plating
Continuing requirements changes
Shortfalls in externally furnished components
Shortfalls in externally performed functions
Real-time performance shortfalls
Straining computer science capabilities

Freedom provides an improved approach.

By precisely defining exactly what constitutes requirements information, Freedom reduces risk associated with incorrect assessment of required functionality (#3) and gold plating (#5), and helps reduce the rate of change of requirements (#6). A more efficient process of requirements discovery, in which the customer or his representative directly assists the requirements specification team, also helps avoid risks #3 through #5. Implementing incorrect functionality (#3) and incorrect user interfaces (#4) are alleviated by requirements recording notations that are directly usable by the implementation team while remaining understandable to the customer. Last, but not least, the unique ability of Freedom to encapsulate requirements in objects greatly reduces the time and cost of changes to requirements (#6) both during development and post-delivery evolution.

The last feature, encapsulation of requirements, is the most important of these improvements. First, requirements encapsulation justifies Freedom. The concept is tacit proof that the methodology offers a different, if not an improved, approach to requirements. No other methodology today captures requirements in a manner that permits their encapsulation in code objects. In fact, no other methodology even recognizes the term "requirements encapsulation." Second, requirements encapsulation offers substantial reductions in the life-cycle cost of software. An estimate of the size of the cost savings that can be expected is given in the last section of this chapter. These savings, which are substantial, indicate that Freedom offers not merely a different approach, but a true improvement in requirements methodology.

1.2 Freedom Methodology Overview

How does Freedom achieve these improvements? What is the "precise" definition of requirements? What is the process, and why is it more efficient? What kind of requirements recording notations are understandable to customers while being directly useful to developers? How does requirements encapsulation work?

To be sure, this book answers these questions and many more. Due to its importance, however, requirements encapsulation deserves an immediate, if brief, overview.

The key to requirements encapsulation is the Requirements Encapsulation Design Rule. Explained in more detail in Chapter 11, this rule states:

> Create one functionality module for each unique stimulus set
> of the functionality tree.

A "functionality module" is an object-oriented (OO) code unit such as a class or object. A "stimulus set" is a cohesive collection of stimuli, or program inputs. A "functionality tree" is a hierarchical organization of stimulus sets. As described in Chapter 7, a functionality tree is also a schematic diagram of the external interface of the software system. Thus, creating a functionality tree involves diagramming the external interface of the software. When software requirements are specified via a functionality tree, they are encapsulatable in code objects via the Requirements Encapsulation Design Rule.

A functionality tree identifies stimuli. Stimuli produce responses. Responses are specified in a set of "behavior tables." These tables record the "meat" of the requirements, that is, the required behavior of the software, in a notation that is directly useful to programmers while remaining readable by the customer. Just as the functionality tree (via the Design Rule) determines which requirements-encapsulating code modules to create, the behavior tables determine what code to write inside each module.

The culminating step of the Freedom requirements process is the development of an external interface mockup. A mockup is a prototype that implements most stimuli but few responses. A mockup also implements the intended protocol, such as the actual look and feel of the human user portion of the interface. The primary purpose of the mockup is to solicit requirements feedback from as many users as possible very early in the development cycle. If the user feedback is favorable, the mockup is not discarded, but is evolved into the final system by incrementally implementing the responses to the stimuli.

The above summarizes what Freedom does. The following summarizes what it does not do.

Freedom is purely a technical development methodology. It provides guidance on how to engineer software but says little about how to manage software projects. For example, Freedom does not address things such as planning, scheduling, cost estimating, personnel organization, reviews, or inspections. Because it includes little management guidance, Freedom is "management neutral"; that is, it supports "separation of technical and management concerns" at the methodology level. Management neutrality permits Freedom to be used with any software management methodology or model such as spiral models, evolutionary and incremental development models, the original waterfall model, people-centric management, document-centric management, and many others.

1.3 Methodology Benefits of Freedom

What is the benefit of methodology separation of concerns? Would a single, full-featured methodology not be superior?

Most will agree that software methodology should vary depending on whether a project is big or small, high or low risk, government or commercial, and so on. However, stability is necessary to realize the economic benefits of software reuse, developer training, tools compatibility, notational conventions, and technical standards. It is noteworthy that the former are management issues whereas the latter are technical in nature. Separation of these concerns allows projects to realize the economic benefits of technical standardization while remaining flexible in management matters. Separation of management and technical concerns is akin to mathematical factoring of an equation. It simplifies the problem, leading to a methodology solution that allows projects to have the best of both worlds.

1.4 Economic Benefits of Freedom

Freedom's benefits are ultimately economic. Using Freedom reduces the time and effort, and therefore the cost, of developing and maintaining software. The total cost reduction is the sum of development and maintenance cost reductions as illustrated in Figure 1.1, and as described below.

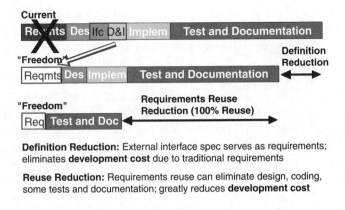

Definition Reduction: External interface spec serves as requirements; eliminates **development cost** due to traditional requirements

Reuse Reduction: Requirements reuse can eliminate design, coding, some tests and documentation; greatly reduces **development cost**

Figure 1.1   Freedom development cost savings.

1.4.1 Development Benefits

Freedom reduces cost during development by precisely defining requirements, being design and implementation neutral, delivering code early, eliminating traceability, and enabling requirements reuse.

Precisely defining requirements reduces cost by ensuring that requirements effort addresses requirements and not design or implementation. Doing the proper work at the proper time results in a more efficient and less costly development process. More importantly, Freedom's definition of requirements implies that a specification of the external interface should serve as the requirements specification. Because the external interface must be specified in any case, Freedom saves cost relative to other methodologies by replacing traditional requirements specifications with the external interface specification. The external interface specification thus does double duty in Freedom, saving cost. As illustrated in Figure 1.1, the resulting cost savings is roughly equal to the cost of developing a traditional requirements specification. One could say that, compared with other methodologies, requirements are free in Freedom!

Design and implementation (D&I) neutrality reduces cost because it reduces the need to think about design and implementation issues when specifying requirements. Requirements in Freedom are D&I neutral because of Freedom's precise, black box-based definition, and because functionality trees and required behavior tables are D&I neutral notations. D&I neutrality complements precise definition of requirements in focusing requirements effort only on requirements, resulting in a more efficient and less costly development process.

Delivering code early reduces cost by obtaining user feedback on the requirements as early as possible. The sooner requirements errors and omissions are discovered, the less time and effort are wasted on products that must be discarded or reworked. Freedom delivers code early in the form of an interface prototype, as described briefly above, and in detail in Chapter 13.

Eliminating traceability reduces the cost that some projects incur maintaining complex traceability mappings between requirements and their implementing code modules. Freedom eliminates any need for traceability maps because encapsulation of requirements in code objects ensures that each requirement (stimulus–response pair) is implemented by one functionality module, as described briefly above and in detail in Chapters 11 and 12. With each requirement mapping to one code module, traceability becomes trivial, and the need to maintain traceability maps is eliminated.

Enabling requirements reuse reduces cost because reusing requirements specifications (functionality trees and behavior tables) and their implementing code modules from previous projects reduces the amount of specification and code that needs to be developed anew on this and subsequent projects. The result can be a substantial decrease in development cost. In the best case, a sufficiently large reusable requirements library could eliminate nearly all design and implementation cost, and perhaps half of the requirements, documentation, and test cost. In this best case, requirements reuse can lower development cost by as much as 68 percent all by itself. The derivation of the 68 percent estimate is given in Appendix B.

1.4.2 Maintenance Benefits

Freedom reduces cost during maintenance by quantifying software quality and encapsulating requirements.

Quantifying software quality reduces cost via metrics for software product and process improvement. As described in Chapter 5, Freedom's quality attributes are quantitative, measured over time while the software is in operation. These measurements provide a basis for product and process improvement, resulting in long-term cost reduction. In addition, the quality attributes are ranked, permitting them to be used as engineering trade-off decision-making criteria. Using ranked objective criteria to make engineering trade-off decisions also helps achieve the customer's quality objectives.

Encapsulating requirements reduces cost by making requirements easier to change throughout the life of the software. Requirements change becomes easier because the code that implements a requirement (stimulus–response pair) is located in a single module, as described in Chapters 11 and 12. In all other methodologies, the code that implements a requirement tends to be scattered among many modules, often in unobvious ways. Thus, changes to code in response to a requirements change is significantly easier with Freedom-architected code than with code architected using other methodologies. Available data indicate requirements encapsulation should lower maintenance cost by 20 percent. The derivation of the 20 percent estimate is given in Appendix B.

1.4.3 Total Economic Benefits

The maximum combined cost reduction due to requirements encapsulation plus requirements reuse (which is enabled by requirements encapsulation) is obtained by combining the development savings and the maintenance savings. This analysis concludes that requirements encapsulation can reduce the total cost of software over its entire life cycle by 16 to 30 percent depending on the extent to which requirements reuse is employed. The derivation of these estimates is given in Appendix B.

The cost savings due to precise definition of requirements, design and implementation neutrality, early delivery of code, elimination of traceability, and quantification of software quality are not included in the above numerical estimates because these savings are more difficult to quantify. When these additional factors are taken into account, the actual cost savings due to using Freedom are likely to be substantially greater than the numbers stated above.

References

1. Brooks, F. 1986. *No Silver Bullet: Essence and Accidents of Software Engineering.* Information Processing '86. New York: Elsevier Science Publishers B.V., page 17.
2. Boehm, B. 1991. *Software Risk Management.* Piscataway, NJ: IEEE Press.

Chapter 2

Information-Hiding Secrets

2.1 Chapter Overview

Freedom requires an understanding of fundamental OO concepts. This chapter briefly reviews the concepts of encapsulation and information-hiding, the elements of OO most relevant to Freedom. During the course of this review, we discover that information-hiding as currently practiced does not fully realize the vision of its inventors. The difference forms the basis for extending OO into the area of requirements, with Freedom being the first methodology to do so.

2.2 Information-Hiding Concepts

Among the most fundamental concepts of OO development are information-hiding and encapsulation. Although the terms are often used synonymously, Freedom distinguishes between the two by the following definitions.

2.2.1 Encapsulation

A technique for improving code maintainability that consists of co-locating cohesive information in a single module and accessing that information only via access programs.

One way to enforce encapsulation of information is to explicitly restrict direct access to the encapsulated information from software external to the module. The restriction may be effected via language syntax or via programmer discipline. The latter fact implies that encapsulation can be achieved using non-OO languages such as C and FORTRAN.[1] Regardless of how access restriction is realized, the concept forms a basis for differentiating encapsulation from information-hiding.

2.2.2 Information-Hiding

> Encapsulation in which direct external access to the hidden information is restricted via syntactical or manual means.

It is very important to remember that the purpose of information-hiding and encapsulation is to improve maintainability of code. It is equally important to realize that the purpose is not to deny information to people; that is, information-hiding and "open source" are not mutually exclusive! Information-hiding is a means of denying other modules direct access to a given module's information. The access-restricted, or "hidden," information can only be accessed by other modules via calls to methods, or "access programs," of the encapsulating module. Information-hiding was never intended to hide information from people.[2]

Forbidding direct programmatic access to data implies that global data are disallowed. A program that is architected to use any global data at all violates information-hiding and encapsulation. Such programs are not object-oriented regardless of whatever other features they may use such as classes, inheritance, or polymorphism. Because most OO languages contain syntax that permits direct access to encapsulated data, non-OO programs can easily be written using OO languages. A true OO program that confers the full maintainability benefits of information-hiding must strictly avoid such permissive syntax.

Why is strict avoidance of direct data access so important to maintainability? The answer requires an understanding of exactly how information-hiding and encapsulation translate to better software maintainability. Here is how it works.

The program being designed is decomposed into parts ("modules") that represent real-world or logical entities (things or "objects" with noun-form names) relevant to the problem being solved. Each module is then designed consistent with Figure 2.1 using a three-step process.

■ Step 1. Identify and hide volatile information. "Volatile" information is data or algorithms for which the implementation details have a

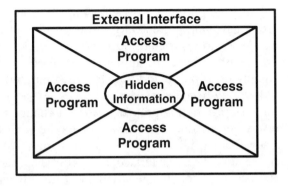

Figure 2.1 **Information-hiding module architecture.**

high probability of change over the life cycle of the program. Such information is identified, and declared in such a way as to make that information inaccessible to other modules. If an object-oriented language such as Java is being used, such data are declared private to the module. If a traditional language such as C or FORTRAN is being used, the data declarations are imported only into the subroutines and functions that comprise the module, but not into any other subprograms. This serves to co-locate and isolate volatile data within their respective modules.

■ Step 2. Create and use access programs. When the algorithms for each module "access program" (Java method, C function, or FORTRAN subroutine) are being written, care is taken to access the volatile data within other modules only via calls to the access programs of those other modules. Intermodule direct data access is strictly avoided; only intramodule direct data access is permitted.

■ *Step 3. Design stable interfaces.* When the interface to each access program is designed, extreme care is taken to define the interface such that the interface details—module name, argument list, argument data types, return data types, and exception or error codes—will have a low probability of change should the encapsulated volatile information change. This defines a "stable" (resilient to change) interface to each module access program.

What does this three-step design approach achieve? Without the three-step design approach, any change to the way a program datum is defined or declared ripples throughout the entire program, affecting each line of code that references the changed datum. Because a datum may be referenced in many different places, possibly under different names, there is a high probability of missing a reference that needs to change and thus introducing a bug into the program. Also, changing all code that references the datum affords many opportunities to introduce new errors. Because adding new capabilities to a program during its life cycle often involves changing the way existing data are implemented, program maintenance is traditionally highly error prone and therefore costly in terms of testing, debugging, multiple bug-fix releases, and so on.

When the three-step design approach is used, a change to a datum is always localized to one module because other modules never reference the datum directly. Rather, all references to the datum are indirect via access programs. The external interface to access programs is stable, meaning the interface does not change when the datum changes. Modules that indirectly reference the datum are not aware the datum has changed because their references are to a stable interface, not to the volatile, changed datum. As a result, when a datum changes, only the code of the module within which it is encapsulated must change; all other modules of the program remain unaffected because of the stable interface. Thus, the ripple effect of the change throughout the program is greatly reduced. This in turn reduces the rate of introduction of new errors, reduces the amount of testing and debugging required, reduces the number of bug-fix releases required, and, in sum total, reduces the time and cost of program evolution and maintenance.

Because as much as 80 percent of a program's cost is accrued during maintenance and evolution of the program,[3] encapsulation (or information-hiding) and stable module interfaces together comprise the most financially beneficial aspect of object-oriented development. Reduction of total life-cycle cost resulting from improved maintainability is why strict avoidance of direct data access is so important.

2.3 Contrast with Traditional Design

Listing 2.1 shows a small Java program that computes the relativistic energy for a given mass using Einstein's famous equation $E = mc^2$. This version of the program is written in the traditional (non-OO) manner. It computes the energy "E" for a value of mass "m" read from the command line, and then prints the value of "E" on the screen. The entire program consists of one small compilation unit named "Einstein."

Rewriting this program using an object-oriented approach can take many forms. One such solution is depicted in Listing 2.2. This OO version of the program also consists of a compilation unit named "Einstein" that accepts the mass value "m" as input from the command line in exactly the same way as the non-OO version. That is, its interface to the user is identical. However, rather than directly encoding the relativistic energy

Listing 2.1   Relativistic Energy Program, Traditional Architecture

```
public class Einstein {
  public static void main (String[ ] args) {
    float m = Float.parseFloat (args[0]);    // read mass from command
                                             line
    float c = 186000.f;                      // set speed of light
    System.out.println ("E = "+(m * c*c));   // compute relativistic
                                             energy

  }
}
```

function, the OO version of "Einstein" calls on two objects to provide the needed functionality.

The first such object is a model of a Physical Object. For our purposes, it need contain values only for mass and equivalent relativistic energy. In our example, both values are set when the mass is set. Individual access programs (Java methods) are defined to access the mass and energy values.

The relativistic energy equation in Physical Object requires the speed of light. Light is the second needed object. On the premise that light is a kind of physical object (i.e., photons), Light is modeled as a subclass of Physical Object having zero mass and one additional property, speed, which is constant. The value for the speed of Light constant is in English units, so the program as a whole is valid only for English units.

The OO version of this simple program is obviously more complex than the non-OO version. Hence, this simple example is not very effective at demonstrating the maintainability advantages of information-hiding, encapsulation, and stable interfaces. These advantages become more pronounced in more-complex programs. The example does, however, clearly indicate that a different way of thinking is involved in designing an OO program, a way of thinking that is centered around objects rather than around formulas or functions. Objects form the conceptual basis for code modules that can be built according to the principles of information-hiding, encapsulation, and stable interfaces.

2.4 Contrast with Current OO Practice

Unfortunately, OO is often improperly practiced. Novice OO programmers often use the permissive data access syntax provided by most OO languages to directly access encapsulated information from outside their modules, thereby violating information-hiding. Many OO developers, including some who are careful to properly information-hide encapsulated data, do not give sufficient attention to design of stable module interfaces.

Listing 2.2   Relativistic Energy Program, OO Architecture

```
public class Einstein {
  public static void main (String[] args) {
    float m = Float.parseFloat (args[0]);       // read mass from
                                                   command line

    PhysicalObject obj = new PhysicalObject();  // create object instance
    obj.setMass (m);                            // set object mass to
                                                   input

    System.out.println (obj.getEnergy());       // get energy of object
  }
}
public class PhysicalObject {                   // model of physical
                                                   object

  private float mass;                           // physical objects have
                                                   mass

  private float energy;                         // and relativistic
                                                   energy

  public void setMass (float mass) {            // interface to set mass
    this.mass = mass;
    this.energy = mass *                        // setting mass also
                                                   changes

      Light.SPEED() * Light.SPEED();            // the relativistic
                                                   energy

  }
  public float getMass ( ) {                    // method to get mass
                                                   value
    return this.mass;
  }
  public float getEnergy ( ) {                  // method to get energy
    return this.energy;
  }
}
public class Light extends PhysicalObject {     // model of Light
  private static final float SPEED = 186000.f;  // light has constant
                                                   speed
  public void setMass (float mass) {            // and zero mass
    super.setMass (0f);
  }
  public static float SPEED ( ) {               // method to get light
                                                   speed

    return SPEED;
  }
}
```

These are common ways in which OO is inadequately practiced, and why its full economic benefits are often not realized.

However, there is at least one other way in which current OO practice is falling short of the vision of the creators of information-hiding.

Information-hiding as a coherent, well-documented concept is the result of the work of the Naval Research Lab's Software Cost Reduction (SCR) project, led by Dr. David Parnas (Figure 2.2). A major report of the SCR project is the "A-7E Software Module Guide."[5] This document organizes the

Figure 2.2   Dr. David L. Parnas.

information-hiding modules of the A-7E aircraft avionics suite into a hierarchical structure based on the types of information encapsulated within the modules. At the top of the hierarchy are three categories, representing three major types of encapsulated information, or module "secrets" as they were called by the SCR team. Although these three categories were identified in the context of an avionics application, they are sufficiently general to apply to all software. The three categories are:

- *Hardware-Hiding Modules.* "Programs that need to be changed if any part of the hardware is replaced." Modules for which the encapsulated information (secret) is "hardware / software interfaces."
- *Required Behavior-Hiding Modules.* "Programs that need to be changed if there are changes in the sections of the requirements document that describe the required behavior." Modules for which the encapsulated information (secret) is "the content of those sections [of the requirements document]."
- *Design Decision-Hiding Modules.* All other programs of the application. Modules for which the encapsulated information (secrets) are "software design decisions based upon mathematical theorems, physical facts, and programming considerations such as algorithmic efficiency and accuracy . . . not described in the requirements document."

Table 2.1   SCR Module Types and Current Practice

SCR Module Type	Current Practice
Hardware-hiding module	Device driver (e.g., operating system)
Design decision-hiding module	Classes and objects encapsulating ■ algorithms ■ data structures
Required behavior-hiding module	NOTHING!

Note that the "A-7E Software Module Guide" was published in 1981, long enough ago to have been forgotten by most software developers today. Yet the lessons it teaches are just as valuable now as they were in 1981. The most important of these lessons is the secrets. Each of the three categories of secrets identified in the "A-7E Software Module Guide" maps to current practice in different ways. This mapping is summarized in Table 2.1, and is described in detail below.

Hardware-hiding modules, which encapsulate interfaces to hardware devices, are now known as "device drivers." Device drivers were the first category of information-hiding module to come into widespread use. Faced with the problem of localizing the ripple effect of changes to hardware peripherals such as printers and monitors, operating system designers discovered the principle of hardware-hiding. Device drivers were one of the first real-world indications that decomposition of systems into modules might best be based on localization of information that may change. However, most operating system designers chose to ignore (or perhaps never realized) that the principle can be applied to more than just interfaces to hardware peripherals. Hence, with the exception of device drivers, most operating systems are still designed today using functional decomposition rather than object-oriented approaches.

Software decision-hiding modules form the basis of modern object-oriented development. Although many types of design decisions can be encapsulated, by far the most common are data structures. Just as operating system designers tend to utilize only hardware encapsulation, many object-oriented developers tend to focus mainly on data structure encapsulation while ignoring (or perhaps not being aware of) other possibilities.

Most important, the vast majority of developers today are totally unaware of the possibility of a third major type of module secret: required behavior encapsulation. A Web search for the terms "requirements encapsulation" and "requirements-hiding" finds very little of relevance (other than Freedom), even though requirements encapsulation was part and parcel of the original concept of information-hiding as documented by the SCR team.

Of the three types of module secrets, required external behavior encapsulation certainly has the highest payoff inasmuch as 80 percent of the changes during 80 percent of the software's life are requirements changes.[3,6] It is therefore logical to conclude that encapsulating (i.e., restricting the ripple effect of changes to) requirements can have a very beneficial impact on software cost. As estimated in Chapter 1, requirements encapsulation has the potential of directly cutting total software cost by 16 percent, with indirect benefits accounting for additional savings.

Were the SCR vision of requirements encapsulation to become standard practice industrywide, the financial benefit to the software industry and its customers could be significant to the point of representing a major advance in software engineering. This substantiates the 1999 opinion of Dr. Parnas that the most promising ideas in software engineering are to properly apply existing techniques.[4] Certainly foremost among these is information-hiding and encapsulation. For the software industry today, the potential cost savings of requirements encapsulation may be the biggest secret of all.

References

1. Lutowski, R.N. 1995. Object-oriented software development with traditional languages. *Fortran Forum* 14: 4 (December).
2. As a software maintainer, my knee-jerk reaction when first hearing the term "information-hiding" was anger. "I need more information, not less! What [bleep] thought of this?!" Later, I learned the true meaning of the term, averting a permanent case of high blood pressure. Apparently, some still retain the knee-jerk belief.
3. Ferens, D.V., Brummert, K.L., and Mischler, Jr, P.R. 1999. A comparative study of model content and parameter sensitivity of software support cost models. In *Proceedings of the 1999 Joint ISPA/SCEA Conference*, San Antonio, TX, June, pp. 1274–1291. Available at http://64.233.167.104/search?q=cache:jZT_rmBQPooJ:www.amc.army.mil/amc/rm/files/ferens_pdss.pdf+80%25+DoD+study+%22software+maintenance+cost%22&hl=en.
4. Eickelmann, N. 1999. ACM fellow profile, David Lorge Parnas. *Software Engineering Notes,* 24: 3 (May).
5. Britton, K.H. and Parnas, D.L. 1981. "A7-E Software Module Guide," NRL Memorandum Report 4702 (December 8), Naval Research Laboratory, Washington, DC.
6. Berry, D.M. 2002. Formal methods: The very idea, some thoughts about why they work when they work. *Science of Computer Programming* 42:1 (January), Figure 3.

Chapter 3

What Are Requirements?

3.1 Chapter Overview

Computers have an annoying trait of forcing us to clarify our thinking before a problem can be automated. Requirements encapsulation is no exception. Before requirements can be encapsulated in code modules, one must clearly understand exactly what is being encapsulated. This chapter addresses the question that is central to both requirements encapsulation and requirements specification: exactly what are requirements?

In the process of precisely defining requirements, precise definitions of "design" and "implementation" also emerge. The precise definitions reveal that some information commonly thought to be requirements turns out not to be. This chapter also discusses how to handle such information.

Freedom's precise definition of requirements is based on the work of the late Dr. Harlan Mills. Mills was an IBM Fellow in addition to being a software engineering research professor. In a 1988 paper,[1] Mills proposed modeling the software system as a black box having behavior described in terms of stimuli and associated responses. According to Mills, such a description of the software system constitutes a "specification that is complete, unambiguous, and consistent." The developers of Freedom recognized the tremendous significance of a complete, unambiguous, and consistent description of the system. Freedom's approach to requirements is a refinement of the initial basic steps outlined in Mills's 1988 paper: first, identify all system stimuli and, second, specify the responses to those stimuli.

> **The black box view of the software system, i.e., those aspects of the software system that are detectable in the external world.**

Figure 3.1 Definition of requirements.

3.2 Definition of Requirements

Prior to Freedom, requirements were defined by statements such as, "What the system shall do but not how it should do it," and "A condition or capability that must be met or possessed by a system to satisfy a contract, standard, or other formally imposed document."[2] The problem with such definitions is they are far too ambiguous to offer useful guidance for encapsulation of requirements. Freedom's definition of requirements is much more technically precise, precise enough to enable requirements encapsulation.

As described previously, the work of the late Dr. Mills provides the critical foundation. Mills was a strong proponent of viewing a software system as a black box, a conceptual model common in many engineering disciplines. Freedom applies Mills' suggestion by defining "requirements" as asserted in Figure 3.1.

A black box is a system view in which the only information known is the information visible or detectable in the external world. Nothing is known about how the system works internally. A ubiquitous example of a black box is a television. For the vast majority of people, the only information known about a television is how to use it; only specialized electrical engineers and repair technicians actually know how one works internally. Similarly, the black box view of a software system is exactly equivalent to the external interface used to operate the software, as illustrated in Figure 3.2. Only specialized software engineers and maintenance personnel need to know how it works internally.

This definition is clearly different from previous notions of requirements. Defining requirements as the black box view of the software system means that requirements are literally the external interface of the software. By this definition, requirements are no longer statements *about* the software recorded in a document; requirements are a *part of* the software.

The notion of the external interface, and only the external interface, being the requirements may be difficult to accept. What possible benefit could be gained by such an unorthodox definition of "requirements"? Also, is not the definition so narrow as to be incomplete?

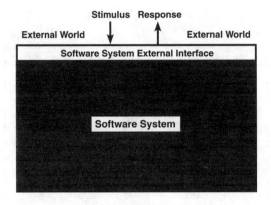

Figure 3.2 Black box model of requirements.

The benefit of the black box definition of requirements stems from the fact that, with requirements defined as the black box view of the system (i.e., its external interface), requirements become encapsulatable. Why? Because interfaces are encapsulatable. Recall that operating system developers have been encapsulating external interfaces to hardware devices using device drivers for decades. Requirements encapsulation simply applies this same strategy to the software system external interface. With requirements encapsulation made possible, the substantial cost savings benefits of requirements encapsulation also become possible.

At the same time, the definition is complete—nothing else need be regarded as requirements—and consistent with previous definitions. Why? Because "what the system shall do" is fully reflected in the system external interface. That is, all capabilities of the system must have some reflection in the external interface. If some do not, those capabilities cannot be invoked and cannot make their results available to the users. Thus, the external interface of the system encompasses 100 percent of what the system can do (external stimuli) as well as 100 percent of the results of the system's doing it (external responses).

If requirements are the external interface, then it follows that a requirements specification is a specification of the external interface. What would such a requirements specification be like? As mentioned earlier, Mills suggested that an external interface can be specified in a "complete, unambiguous, and consistent" manner by describing the stimulus–response behavior of the system. Freedom therefore specifies the software system interface in terms of system external stimuli and associated external responses, plus the external protocols. The protocols include the "look and feel" for the interface to humans, and detailed communication formats for interfaces to external systems and the environment.

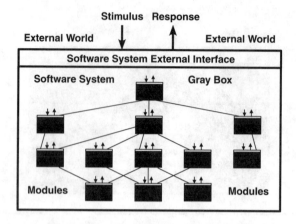

Figure 3.3   Gray box model of design.

In summary, a requirements (i.e., external interface) specification consists of:

1. All external stimuli of the system
2. All associated external responses
3. All external communication protocols

Significant cost savings and complete, unambiguous, and consistent requirements specification are just the beginning of the changes that result from the black box definition of requirements. The entire software development process is affected, including the definitions of "design" and "implementation."

3.3 Definition of Design

With requirements defined as the black box, or external, view of the system, it follows that the definition of design has to do with the internal view of the system.

When we peek inside a software system black box, what do we see? The answer is: more black boxes, as depicted in Figure 3.3. Each of these internal black boxes represents one code module, such as a Java or C++ class. Because the system black box contains more black boxes, Freedom calls this the "gray box" view of the software system.[3] This "color" terminology is reflected in the definition of "design" as asserted in Figure 3.4.

In a manner analogous to requirements, the definition of design implies that the gray box view of a software system includes the stimulus–response

> **The gray box view of the software system, i.e., those aspects of the software system that lie within the software system black box but outside the black boxes of the individual modules.**

Figure 3.4   Definition of design.

> **The white box view of the software system, i.e., those aspects of the software system that lie within the module black boxes.**

Figure 3.5   Definition of implementation.

behavior and the detailed communication protocols of the module black boxes. Thus, a design specification consists of the following.

1. Identification of each module black box and (assuming all modules are information-hiding modules) their encapsulated information
2. Identification of the relationships among the module black boxes
3. Specification of the module stimuli
4. Specification of the response behavior for each module stimulus
5. Specification of the detailed communication protocols that comprise the stable interfaces to the modules

3.4 Definition of Implementation

With requirements defined as the black box view of the software system and design as the gray box view, it naturally follows that "implementation" is defined as asserted in Figure 3.5.

Figure 3.6 illustrates the white box[4] view, which is what we see when we peek inside the individual module black boxes. What is revealed, of course, is the complete module source code.

As we show in Chapter 4, Freedom is lenient with regard to process details. Freedom permits, and even encourages, tailoring the Freedom process to a given project providing the process remains consistent with the definitions of implementation, design, and, most important, requirements. These definitions lie at the core of Freedom. Just as violation of encapsulation and information-hiding compromises OO, violation of the

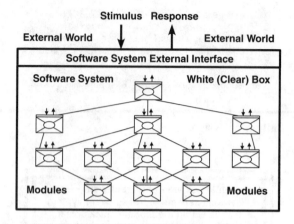

Figure 3.6   White box model of implementation.

definitions of requirements, design, and implementation compromise Freedom.

3.5 Design and Implementation Constraints

How does one reconcile the black box definition of requirements with the traditional requirements definition of "A condition or capability that must be met or possessed by a system to satisfy a . . . formally imposed document?" Those who pay the bills are free to contractually specify whatever they want. What do we do when the customer contractually specifies design or implementation information under the banner of "requirements"? Are not those who pay the bills free to ask for whatever they want, regardless of definitions adopted by the development team? Imagine the following conversation.

> Customer: Also, our requirements state the code shall be written using the Freedom requirements encapsulation technique. We want all the requirements encapsulated in code modules so we can save money on maintenance.

> Prospective Contractor: I am very familiar with Freedom. For example, I know Freedom says that code details are not requirements, by definition. If you want us to use Freedom, you must rewrite the requirements to remove anything that talks about code details, including requirements being encapsulated in code modules. All you can specify as requirements are the external interface and its stimulus–response behavior.

Customer: Thanks for that insight. I think we will change the requirements and remove the part about using Freedom. Also, this interview is over. . . . Next candidate.

The dilemma in the above nightmare scenario is easily handled. Customers can specify anything they want as contractual requirements. The development team, being cognizant of Freedom's technical definition of requirements, treats contractually mandated design and implementation information as "design and implementation constraints," or D&I constraints for short. Because the customer specified them, D&I constraints have the same contractual weight as true black box requirements. However, the technical team keeps D&I constraints separate from the true requirements. For example, in any requirements documentation delivered to the customer by the development team, D&I constraints appear in their own chapter or section separate from the black box requirements.

The difference is more than just academic for the following two reasons:

1. Tagging information appropriately as D&I constraints reminds the developers that this information is technically not requirements, and is therefore not subject to requirements encapsulation. (Some D&I constraints may be encapsulatable as design decision or hardware interface information, and some may not be encapsulatable at all.)
2. Labeling appropriate information as D&I constraints signals the customer that these parts of the contract limit the design and implementation choices available to the developers, perhaps forcing delivery of a system that does not meet the quality requirements as well (see Chapter 5, Quality Requirements).

For this last reason, D&I constraints should be avoided unless specifically requested by the customer for a compelling reason.

References

1. Mills, H. 1988. Stepwise refinement and verification in box-structured systems. *IEEE Computer* 21:6 (June), pages 23–36.
2. *IEEE Glossary of Software Engineering Terminology.* 1990. IEEE Std 610.12.
3. Mills called this the "state box" view of the system but, in keeping with the color metaphor, Freedom uses the term "gray box."
4. Mills called this implementation the "clear box" view because no unknown information remains once the code is in hand. This is perhaps a better description than white box view, but Freedom uses the term "white box" simply for consistency with the color metaphor.

Chapter 4

Freedom Requirements Process

4.1 Chapter Overview

In order to enable encapsulation of requirements, the Freedom requirements process is different from that of other methodologies. The focus is not on use cases, scenario descriptions, or process diagrams. Rather, the emphasis is on specification and prototyping of the software system external interface. However, prior to specification of the external interface, process diagrams—in the forms of enterprise process models and context diagrams—do come into play as prerequisites to the Freedom requirements process. Common to both of these prerequisite process diagrams is the software system black box, which lies within the enterprise model and is central to the context diagram. The proper progression is:

Enterprise model → software black box bounding → context diagram → requirements process.

Each of these processes is discussed in this chapter, in the order shown above. Subsequent chapters focus on individual steps of the requirements process and associated concepts.

Another process, called build versus buy, is performed after development of the context diagram and before the requirements process. As a peer to the requirements process, build versus buy is outside the scope of this book, but is described in other Freedom information sources.

4.2 Enterprise Process Models

Before automating a task or process, a model of the customer's current mission or business process should first be developed. Usually this will be done as part of the customer's process improvement strategy when determining the cost–benefit to the customer of additional software. In some cases, however, the customer may not have a formal process improvement initiative, or the requisite strategic analysis may not have been performed for whatever reason. In this case, the portion of the customer's current mission or business process most relevant to the new software should be modeled with the assistance of the software development team prior to developing the requirements for the software to be built.

4.3 Bounding the Black Box

In terms of an enterprise process model, a software system black box represents a set of tasks to be automated, the development of which will be managed separately from other sets of tasks. Where to draw the software black box boundaries within the enterprise model is a decision for customer management because management factors such as how many software development contractors are to be employed, how the total effort is to be funded and controlled, and how risks are to be mitigated, are relevant.

Because Freedom defines requirements as the black box view of the software, what constitutes requirements for the software depends heavily on where management draws the black box boundaries. Consider, for example, two scenarios for a simple client-server software system.

In Scenario 1, customer management decides to manage development of both server and client-side systems as one application developed by a single team and funded as a single project. In this case, the requirements for the system would be equivalent to that of the client system. Interfaces between the client and server components would be design and implementation information inasmuch as these interfaces lie within the black box boundary.

In Scenario 2, management decides to assign the client software to one team, the server software to a second team, and to manage the development as two interacting projects. In this case, interfaces between the client and server become requirements information for both teams. In addition, requirements for the client team include same client external interfaces as in Scenario 1.

Thus, the content of the requirements documents is implicitly determined by customer management at the time the black box boundaries are defined. The development team is constrained to explicitly identifying, detailing, and recording the requirements (external interfaces) that were implicitly defined by customer management when the boundaries of the black box were drawn within the enterprise model.

4.4 Context Diagrams

A context diagram depicts the entire process being modeled as a single task, or box, in a process diagram. The purpose of a context diagram is to identify all external sources of input, and all external destinations for output, of the software system. This includes input and output to human users, external systems, and the physical environment. The sources and destinations of input and output are called "actors." Each actor in a context diagram is represented as a separate box that interacts with the software system. The interactions are shown as arrows to and from the actor box and the software system box, with the arrows representing information sent by the actor to the software (stimuli), or by the software to the actor (responses).

One of the best ways to create a context diagram is to start with the black box boundaries defined by management on the enterprise model. Extract from the enterprise model the black box and all task boxes with which it connects, ignoring the remainder of the enterprise model. Place the black box representing the software to be developed in the center of the context diagram, and arrange the task boxes around it. Each interacting box is an actor. Represent actors that are other software systems with boxes, and actors that are manual processes with a symbol representing a human. Identify and add other actors that may not appear on the enterprise model, including human users, aspects of the physical environment with which the software must interact, and external systems, files, and databases not shown on the enterprise model. Draw arrows between each actor and the software black box depicting stimuli and responses, and label each arrow to identify the type of information being passed.

An example of a context diagram is that for the overall Freedom process, shown in Figure 4.1. The single box representing the Freedom process has arrows connecting it to relevant external entities including customer management, users, vendors, developers, reusable software component libraries, and the customer enterprise model being automated. The single box representing the process of interest in a context diagram is usually decomposed into more detailed process diagrams. For example, the box labeled "Freedom" in Figure 4.1 decomposes into a Freedom life-cycle process diagram, which in turn decomposes into individual task diagrams such as the Freedom requirements process. This multilevel decomposition is illustrated in Figure 4.2.

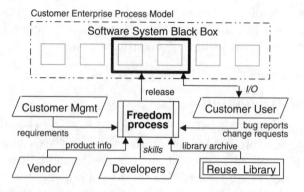

Figure 4.1   Freedom context diagram.

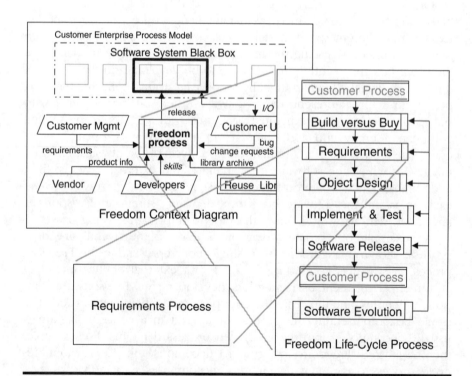

Figure 4.2   Freedom process decomposition.

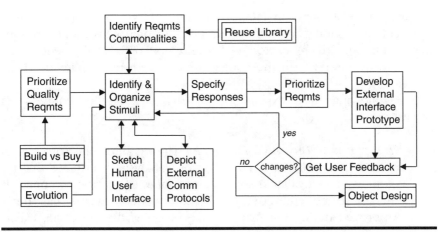

Figure 4.3   Freedom requirements process.

4.5 Requirements Process

The Freedom requirements process is illustrated by the process diagram of Figure 4.3. The primary purpose of the requirements process is to provide guidance for developers tasked with specifying the requirements of the software to be developed. The Freedom requirements process diagram does not depict a step-by-step procedure to be followed rigorously. Rather, it documents a "rational process" as defined by Parnas and Clements.[1]

Briefly, a rational process is a process that need not be followed rigorously. Rather, one can do whatever it takes to get the job done providing the results produced appear as if the documented process were followed. That is, the process diagram does not define a procedure to be followed, but a set of products to be produced. The process steps can be "faked" providing the correct products are produced. Thus, Freedom doesn't really care how a functionality tree, behavior tables, and other products specified by the Freedom process chart are produced. Freedom only cares that they are produced because requirements encapsulation and other aspects of Freedom rely on these notations.

It is essential that the requirements process be carried out with the direct participation of the customer or a designated representative, referred to by Freedom as the customer Point of Contact (POC). The POC must be a subject matter specialist in the domain of the software to be developed, and must sufficiently understand the customer's needs and desires for the required software. Although referred to in this discussion in the singular, the POC may, in fact, be a body of two or more customer representatives should more than one be available to assist the development team. Any reference to the "developers" or "development team" anywhere in this book in the context of requirements implies the POC as well.

The following is an explanation of each task of the requirements process.

- *Build versus Buy and Evolution.* The requirements process is entered only after a *build versus buy* analysis determines that no commercially available software can meet the customer's need. It may also be entered after a requirements change has been approved during the maintenance phase of the life cycle, called Evolution by Freedom.

- *Prioritize Quality Requirements.* The default quality attribute ranking, given in Chapter 5, is modified to reflect the customer's quality priorities for the software to be developed. In many cases, the default ranking will be adequate and no modification will be necessary. A list of the customer-ranked quality requirements is given to each member of the development team, and posted prominently in cubicles, meeting rooms, and anywhere else where software development decisions may be made.

- *Identify and Organize Stimuli.* The first step when specifying capability requirements in terms of stimulus–response behavior is to identify and organize stimuli. Stimuli are identified for each source of input identified in the context diagram (described above). Rough specification of the protocol for each source helps to identify stimuli. Simultaneously, stimuli are organized and recorded using a functionality tree, a notation that organizes stimuli based on their activation dependencies. As explained in Chapter 7, a functionality tree defines the architecture of the external interface. Identification and organization of stimuli into a functionality tree is the central task of the requirements process, as indicated in Figure 4.3 by the mass of arrows intersecting this task.

- *Sketch Human User Interface.* Stimulus identification is aided in part by development of functionality screens, which depict in rough form the look and feel of the human user part of the software external interface. Described in Chapter 6, Section 6.4, functionality screens are often a good place to start because most customer personnel relate easily to pictures of the human user interface. Stimuli, in the form of buttons, data entry fields, and the like are easy to identify in these sketches.

- *Depict External Communication Protocols.* Stimulus identification is aided in part by development of communication protocols to external systems, including files and external databases, and the environment. Such protocols typically consist of sequential streams of commands and data, as described in Chapter 8. The format of the command-data streams are often the responsibility of external organizations, in which case this task is one of requesting information from others, then organizing it into a functionality tree.
- *Identify Requirements Commonalities.* As the functionality tree is developed, repetitions in the tree are sometimes observed. As described in Chapter 6, Section 6.5, these repetitions or commonalities in the functionality tree often indicate reusable requirements components. Recorded using a simple referential name, reusable requirements components simplify the functionality tree, the application code, and, most importantly, future applications.
- *Reuse Library.* Reusable requirements components created on this and other projects are stored in the reuse library. The library is inspected for requirements components that may be of use in the current application. Any that are found are inserted into the functionality tree by reference.
- *Specify Responses.* After the stimuli have been identified and organized into a functionality tree, the response behavior for each stimulus is specified using behavior tables, as described in Chapter 10. The emphasis is on externally detectable parts of the responses, consistent with the definition of requirements. Any design and implementation constraints are also recorded in the behavior tables, but are segregated from the external responses that specify true requirements. Behaviors of all types are recorded using Program Design Language (PDL). PDL consists of structured natural language that is readable by customer personnel, yet sufficiently structured and logical to be comfortable and clear to programmers.
- *Prioritize Requirements.* If desired by the customer, the requirements stimuli may be prioritized based on importance or immediacy of need. Requirements priorities take the form of annotations to the functionality tree, as described in Chapter 9. The highest priority stimuli are included in the current release, and lower priorities in subsequent releases. Stimulus priorities form the basis for incremental development. Waterfall and other nonincremental development models are easily supported by making all stimuli equal priority, that is, not assigning priorities.
- *Develop External Interface Prototype.* The functionality screens illustrating the look and feel of the human user interface, and the

command-data streams depicting interfaces to external systems and the environment, are refined and verified by development of an interface mockup. As described in Chapter 13, an interface mockup is release quality code that implements most stimuli, but few responses. It is used to obtain user feedback on the requirements, especially identification of errors and omissions, very early in the development process when corrections are least expensive to make. Interface mockups have been shown to be highly effective in practice[2] as a means of verifying the stimuli.

■ *Get Customer Feedback.* The interface mockup is delivered to the customer for evaluation and approval. At the same time, a heuristic evaluation[3] or other form of usability inspection[4] may be carried out by the development test team or a specialized usability contractor hired by the customer. The primary purpose of a heuristic evaluation or other usability inspection is to improve the usability of the human user interface. Any requirements stimuli, protocol, and usability concerns are addressed by revising the functionality tree, behavior tables, functionality screens, and other protocol specifications. The interface mockup is then revised and re-evaluated until the users and usability inspectors are satisfied.

■ *Object Design.* The output of the requirements process is input to the object design process. This output specifies the capability requirements as recorded in the functionality tree, associated behavior tables, functionality screens, and other protocol specifications. These notations and their relationships are depicted graphically in Figure 4.4.

Starting with object design, the user-verified interface prototype is grown into the final system by incrementally adding response behavior according to the requirements priorities. As the response behavior code is designed and implemented, validation tests are written and used to ensure the code conforms to the required behavior.

4.6 Example Problem Enterprise Process Model

By way of example, assume a hypothetical furniture manufacturing company called Furmasco (short for Furniture Manufacturing & Sales Co.) Furmasco sells directly to consumers via their mail-order catalogue, which reduces the high cost of furniture retailing and showrooms. The company is organized around its catalogue-based sales approach, and the six business units are well-entrenched by tradition.

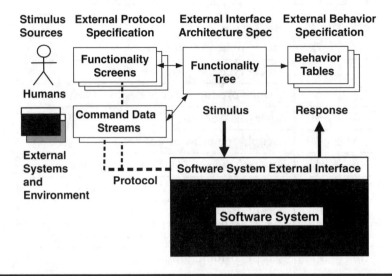

Figure 4.4 Capability requirements notations.

- Dept. D: Development—designs and builds the furniture
- Dept. F: Finance—handles all monetary matters
- Dept. IT: Information Technology—manages all computer hardware and software
- Dept. M: Marketing—markets and advertises the furniture
- Dept. O: Ordering—deals with customer orders and customer service
- *Dept. S: Shipping*—ships the furniture and manages the inventory

Not surprisingly, Furmasco management decides to supplement the catalogue sales by selling their furniture via the Web. With the help of the IT department, management develops an enterprise model of their proposed Web-based sales operation. They start by identifying tasks for each department, listing them in nominal order of performance. Eventually, the list grows to the 23 tasks listed in Table 4.1. The task dependencies are then further clarified by drawing an enterprise process flow model. When drawing the enterprise model, the tasks assigned to a given business unit are kept as close together as possible on the diagram. The model is then distributed for review and comment to all affected business units. After resolution of the review comments and questions, the final model takes the form shown in Figure 4.5. Some notable features of the final enterprise model include:

Table 4.1   **Example Problem Enterprise Model Tasks**

Seq.	Dept.	Task
1	D	Create or acquire products
2	I	Create Web site pages
3	S	Change products and prices in database
4	M	Advertise Web site
5	I	Accept Web browser connections to Web site
6	I	Service browser 2-D Web page requests
7	I	Service browser 3-D Web page requests
8	O	Accept product selections for purchase
9	O	Display selected products and prices
10	O	Accept customer information
11	O	Accept credit card information
12	F	Verify credit card information
13	O	Accept order request
14	O	Assign order number
15	O	Display order receipt
16	O	Process order
17	F	Bill credit card company for payment
18	M	Add customer to e-mail list
19	F	Accept credit card payment
20	S	Ship products
21	M	E-mail product ads to customer list
22	I	Service e-mail remove request
23	M	Remove customer from e-mail list

1. An online database of all current furniture products and prices
2. Online communication with credit card verification and billing services
3. An option for displaying furniture products in 3-D virtual reality
4. Advertising via e-mail (legal in the United States if the user is given the option of being removed from the e-mail list).

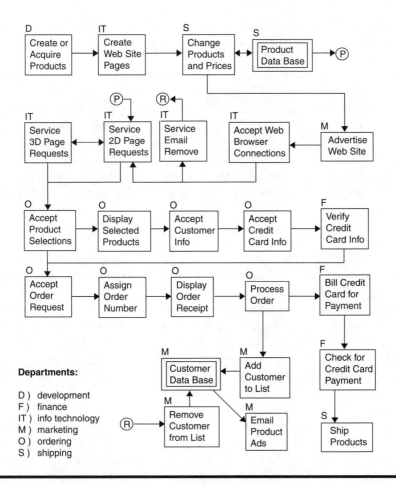

Figure 4.5 Example problem enterprise model.

4.7 Example Problem Black Box Bounding

The next step for Furmasco management in its pursuit of online furniture sales is to identify the necessary software initiatives. The enterprise model proves very useful for this planning.

The planning starts by identifying tasks that will not require new Web-based software, but will continue to be performed using existing methods. Management identifies four such tasks which are, paradoxically, labeled "manual" even though all currently rely on software to some extent. These are: create or acquire products, create Web site pages, advertise Web site, and ship products. The remaining 19 tasks require acquisition of new software.

Next, management determines if any tasks can make use of off-the-shelf software. Two such tasks are identified:

1. *Accept Web browser connections.* Management immediately recognizes that Web servers exist to fulfill this function.
2. *Service 3-D page requests.* IT discovers the JReality "CM Surveyor" 3-D browser, an applet that extends conventional Web browsers to display 3-D virtual reality Web pages.

Management also suggests that the "Service 2-D page requests" and the "Service e-mail remove" tasks might also be handled by the Web servers. IT points out that Web servers service both static Web pages and pages dynamically generated using CGI scripts or Java servlets. Therefore, these tasks actually imply writing the scripts or servlets for the dynamic pages, as well as selecting and configuring an appropriate app server. Thus, only two tasks can be handled by off-the-shelf software, leaving 17 tasks in need of new custom software.

Although there are many ways in which the 17 tasks could be grouped into independent cooperating software projects, management decides to leverage the existing, and successful, business unit structure of the company. Five black box boundaries are drawn on the enterprise model, as shown in Figure 4.6. Each black box defines a software initiative for a business unit owning tasks to be automated.

1. *Credit card Web services.* The finance department will manage development of a credit card verification and billing system. The system will use Web services to interface with a credit card services company, and will provide a custom internal interface for use by order processing and shipping.
2. *App server system.* IT will be responsible for the aforementioned dynamic Web page generation code, app and Web server selection, as well as "manual" creation of static Web pages including the virtual reality pages for display by CM Surveyor.
3. *Marketing system.* Marketing will expand their customer list to include e-mail addresses, and will be in charge of developing the e-mail advertising system. The marketing system will interface with the app server for e-mail removal requests, and with the order processing system for addition of new customer data.
4. *Order processing system.* The order processing system will incorporate the actual business logic behind the online sales Web pages. It will interface with the credit card and marketing systems as well as with the app server. Of course, its development will be managed by the order processing department.

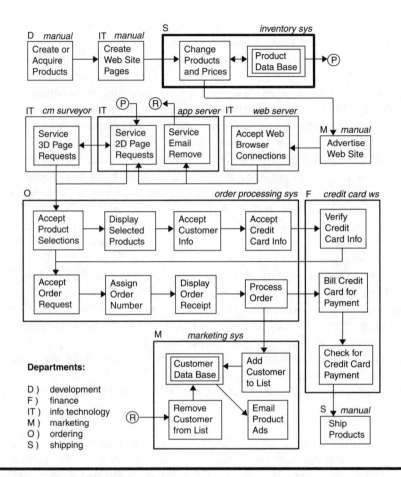

Figure 4.6   Example problem black box bounds.

5. *Inventory system*. The product database maintained by shipping will provide the latest product information to the app server system in support of dynamic page generation, and also to marketing for advertising.

A disagreement arises in the context of the inventory system. The current product database, being one of the first automation projects at Furmasco, uses a proprietary inventory package running on an old 1980s vintage minicomputer. Obtaining support for both the hardware and software has been a problem. With management's approval, shipping decides to take advantage of the new Web initiative to replace the entire inventory system. However, shipping finds the cost of commercial inventory systems to be high. Because their needs are modest, shipping believes that for nearly the same cost they can develop their own inventory system, avoiding the annual cost of a service contract, and the usual problems of proprietary software. IT points out that 80 percent of the cost of a system is in maintenance, even if developed internally, so the cost savings argument is ill-founded, although there are benefits to having access to the code. Management suggests that the Freedom methodology might offer a solution inasmuch as it purports to reduce maintenance cost by as much as 20 percent via encapsulation of requirements. At the very least, detailed requirements can be developed very quickly using Freedom, and can then serve as a basis for a better estimate of the development cost. Shipping agrees to develop requirements for the new inventory system using Freedom, and then re-evaluate the alternatives.

IT mentions that defining black boxes based on department boundaries appears consistent with the "software fortress" model; perhaps the five software systems could be architected as software fortresses.[5] Management agrees to consider it, but also wants to see what shipping says about Freedom. If they like it, perhaps the project initiatives can all use Freedom. After all, the cost of so many new software development tools and methods on different projects has been reducing dividends to the shareholders. It would be nice to find a software approach that, for once, saves money rather than spends more of it. Wouldn't *that* be a switch! Maybe Freedom and fortresses could be used together.[6]

In summary, applying an enterprise model requires management to do the following.

1. Identify all corporate tasks in the domain of interest.
2. Develop an enterprise process model diagram for the tasks.
3. Determine which tasks require new software to be acquired.
4. Determine which of those tasks can be handled by off-the-shelf software.
5. Draw one or more black boxes around the remaining tasks, with each black box representing a separately managed custom software initiative.

4.8 Example Problem Context Diagram

With shipping tasked to develop its requirements using Freedom, our examples henceforth focus on the inventory system.

Because Freedom requirements are external interface-centric, shipping's first task is to identify all the external interfaces to their system by creating a context diagram. The black box bounded enterprise model is

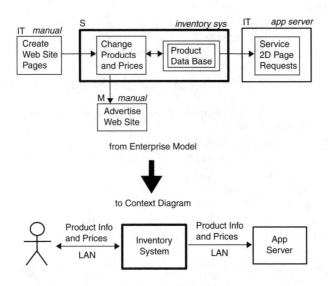

Figure 4.7 Example problem context diagram creation.

a natural starting point. It is a simple matter to strip away all irrelevant parts of the enterprise model and focus only on the inventory system and the tasks with which it interfaces. This stripped enterprise model is then easily converted to a context diagram, as illustrated in Figure 4.7.

First, the inventory system is represented as a single black box; that is, internal details are hidden. Next, manual tasks are replaced by a human actor icon, and external automated systems are represented by other black boxes with their details hidden also. Finally, and most importantly, arrows representing interfaces to these external entities are drawn and labeled to identify the types of information that flow over the interfaces. The simple inventory system envisioned by shipping has only two interfaces.

The first is a human user interface for use by themselves and IT to enter new product data into the database, and for use by marketing to query product data for advertising. This access will be via a traditional desktop application over a local area network (LAN) offline from the Web, a security expedient permitted by the fact that Furmasco manufactures all its furniture at its central home office and plant. All catalogues and other marketing materials are also printed at the home office.

The second is a programmatic interface that permits the app server to query for product and price information to support dynamic Web page generation. Because the servers will be located at the home office, this access will also be via a secure LAN.

References

1. Parnas, D.L. and Clements, P.C. 1986. A rational design process: How and why to fake it. *IEEE Transactions on Software Engineering* SE-12:2 (February), 251–257.
2. Gibbs, W.W. 1997. Command and control. *Scientific American* (August), 33–34.
3. Hom, J. 1996. Heuristic evaluation. Web page, available at http://jthom.best. vwh.net/usability/heuristic.htm.
4. Nielsen, J. 1995. Usability inspection methods. In *CHI '95 Proceedings Tutorials,* Web page, available at http://www.acm.org/sigchi/chi95/proceedings/tutors/jn_bdy.htm.
5. Sessions, R. 2003. *Software Fortresses—Modeling Enterprise Architectures.* Reading, MA: Addison-Wesley.
6. They can. Freedom pairs well with many different methodologies and approaches.

Chapter 5

Quality Requirements

5.1 Chapter Overview

The definition of requirements as "the black box view of a software system" encompasses two different types of information. One of these is referred to by Freedom as "quality requirements." As illustrated in Figure 5.1, quality requirements should be the first requirements specified for any project. This chapter reveals why this is so by explaining what quality requirements are, and how they are used to endow and measure software quality. The respective roles of the customer and developer relative to software quality are also examined.

5.2 Types of Requirements

Two types of requirements information are inherent in the black box view of a software system:

1. *Capability Requirements.* Specific capabilities provided by the stimulus–response behavior of the external system interface. Also called "Functionality Requirements."
2. *Quality Requirements.* Measurable attributes of the software system as a whole, ranked to reflect their relative importance to the customer.

An example of a capability requirement is the stimulus–response behavior of a single button. An example of a quality requirement is usability,

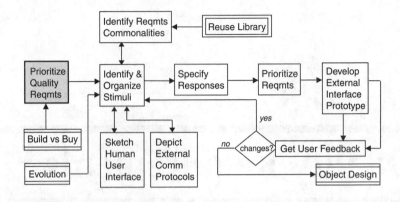

Figure 5.1   Quality requirements in the requirements process.

Table 5.1   Quality versus Capability Requirements

Quality Requirement	Capability Requirement
Specified by quality attribute ranking	Specified by stimulus–response
Serve as trade-off selection criteria	Serve as system completion criteria
Responsibility of *all* modules	Responsibility of *one* module
Measured after release	Verified before release
Measured over a period of time	Verified by discrete tests
Example: usability	Example: one button

or the time to perform a task, in which pressing the button may be only a single step. Capability and quality requirements are similar in that both are black box (or externally detectable) information. However, in most other respects such as utility, traceability, and measurement, they are very different as evidenced by Table 5.1.

■ *Utility.* Capability requirements serve as development completion criteria; that is, a release is complete when all capability requirements assigned to the release have been implemented, tested, and documented. Quality requirements, on the other hand, are used as technical trade-off selection criteria. For example, quality requirements are the criteria by which developers evaluate and choose among competing algorithm or data structure alternatives.

■ *Traceability.* Capability requirements are the responsibility of specific code modules. Quality requirements cannot be traced to any specific code module, but are attributes of the software system as

Table 5.2 Standard Quality Attributes

Rank	Quality Attribute	Actor Served	Software Metric
1	Functionality	User	Percentage of requirements met
2	Reliability	User	Mean time to recover (MTTR)
3	Usability	User	Time to learn Time to perform tasks
4	Administerability	System admin.	Time to install and configure
5	Maintainability	Maintainer	Mean time to upgrade or repair
6	Execution speed	Computer	Run time (beyond requirements)
7	Storage demand	Computer	Units of memory and mass storage

a whole. For example, there is no single module that provides reliability; all modules must be reliable if the system as a whole is to be reliable.

▪ *Measurement.* Capability requirement conformance can be measured by discrete tests prior to release. Quality requirement metrics are measured by monitoring the software in production after release. For example, a measure of reliability is mean time to recover, which is measured by averaging downtime per failure over a substantial period of time.

5.3 Measuring Software Quality

The quality requirements for a software system consist of seven quality attributes along with rankings that reflect their relative importance to the customer for the system being developed. Each of the quality attributes serves a specific actor within the customer organization, and is measured using a software metric specific to that attribute, as shown in Table 5.2. Each quality attribute has a default ranking, which may be adjusted for any given software project as necessary. The seven quality requirements in default rank order are:

1. *Functionality.* The ability of a system to perform its intended function in the environment specified for its usage. Measured by the percentage of capability requirements met (ideally 100 percent).

Default ranked #1 because providing required functionality is the reason a program exists.

2. *Reliability*. The probability that a system will perform its intended functions over a time interval. Measured by mean time to recover (MTTR).[1] Default ranked #2 because if a system is unreliable or unavailable it may not be able to perform its intended function when needed.

3. *Usability*. The amount of time required for a user to make a system perform its intended functions. Measured by average time to learn, and average time to perform specific tasks. Default ranked #3 because a program that is hard to use may preclude users from taking full advantage of its functionality, may adversely affect user productivity, or may even be actively avoided by users.

4. *Administerability*. The amount of time that a system administrator must spend maintaining the system on all the platforms for which she is responsible. Examples are average time to install and configure, and average time per month that the system requires the active attention of an administrator. Default ranked #4 because a program that is difficult to install or administer may result in a system administrator not being able to install or configure it properly, thereby compromising some of its functionality, or perhaps making the program unavailable for use at all.

5. *Maintainability*. The average amount of time required for a maintainer to effect a change to a system. Measured by average time to upgrade (enhance) or repair (fix bugs). Default ranked #5 because the labor cost of maintenance is generally higher than the hardware cost of speed or storage, but is generally less significant than the economics of day-to-day usage inherent in reliability and usability.

6. *Execution Speed*. The ability of a system to respond at speeds in excess of those specified by the capability requirements. Measured by average time per operation. Default ranked #6 because of the continually decreasing cost of machine cycles. However, more speed can translate to improved economics of use, making speed more important than storage demand.

7. *Storage Demand*. The ability of a system to reside in less storage than that specified by the capability requirements. Measured by maximum bytes of storage needed during operation. Default ranked #7 because of the continually decreasing cost of storage, including both volatile (e.g., RAM) and persistent (e.g., disk or tape) storage.

As pointed out above and summarized in Table 5.2, these attributes are all quantitative in nature. However, they all must be measured over time after the software is placed in operational use, as indicated in Table 5.1. Thus, precise determination of software quality cannot be known until well after the software is released and development contractors have left for other jobs. Therefore, unless the software is developed in-house, developers may never know exactly how good a job they did qualitywise. In the case of serious problems they will, of course, know how poor a job they did! Such is the ironic nature of software quality.

5.4 Where's the Developer?

As shown in Table 5.2, each of the seven quality attributes exists to serve a specific actor in the customer organization. The customer actors most directly affected by software quality are users, system administrators, maintainers, and those concerned with procuring additional customer computer hardware.

1. *Users.* Customer personnel who will actually use the program. Users are served by the Functionality, Reliability, and Usability quality attributes.
2. *System Administrators.* The system administration staff of the customer IT department. Served by the administerability quality attribute.
3. *Maintainers.* Customer personnel, or designated subcontractors, who maintain the software system after release. They may be identical to the original development staff, at least for an initial (usually relatively short) period of time. Maintainers are served by the Maintainability quality attribute.
4. *Computer Procurement.* Customer personnel who enhance the hardware systems on which the software will be hosted. Served by the Execution Speed and Storage Demand attributes because good performance and efficient storage utilization can delay or eliminate the need to upgrade the hardware.

One actor conspicuous by his absence in the above list is our good friend, the developer. Why is the developer missing?

The answer is that quality requirements relate to actors who are affected *by* software quality. Quality requirement actors are consumers of quality. The role of developers is to provide quality, not consume it. A developer is responsible not only for ensuring the software meets the capability requirements, but for ensuring it best meets the quality requirements as well. Developers must consistently choose in favor of the customer's needs for quality whenever alternate solutions or approaches present themselves.

Doing so may require that developers sacrifice things such as tools that speed and ease development, technically elegant solutions, or the latest cool technology when such things compromise the quality requirements. The customer's needs for quality are paramount, and supersede the developer's desires for a quick, easy, exciting, and fun development experience. Because quality implications are inherent with every development decision, small or large, the quality requirements must be kept foremost in mind by each member of the development team at all times. Developers' natural inclinations to make decisions that ease their own work must be suppressed in favor of decisions based on the customer-ranked quality requirements.

Eschewing one's own needs is not easy. The sign of a high-quality developer is one who produces software that meets both the capability and quality needs of the customer. Such a developer is not found in the list of quality requirement actors, but is high in the "call first" list of customers. A call for follow-on work is a contract developer's measure of software quality.

5.5 'ility Mapping

There are many "ilities" that can serve as quality requirements other than the seven listed above. However, most if not all of these other attributes fall into the scope of the seven standard quality attributes. Hence, the seven standard quality attributes alone are usually sufficient. Table 5.3 helps verify this "completeness" premise by identifying 18 lower-level quality attributes, and mapping them to the seven standard quality attributes. As an aid to understanding the lower-level attributes and the mapping, definitions for these attributes are given in the table.

5.6 Example Problem Quality Requirements

After developing the context diagram for the Furmasco furniture inventory system, the shipping department development team, consisting of selected personnel from IT and shipping, determines the quality attribute ranking appropriate for the inventory project. They do this by re-evaluating the criteria underlying the default ranking from the standpoint of their project.

5.6.1 Functionality

Default ranked #1 because providing required functionality is the reason a program exists.

Table 5.3 Low-Level Quality Attribute Mapping

Standard Attributes	Lower-Level Attributes	Description
Functionality	Completeness	The degree to which a system implements all of its required capabilities; i.e., percentage of stimulus sets implemented
	Correctness	The degree to which a system conforms to its required response specifications; i.e., percentage of code modules that conform to behavior table specifications as measured by validation tests
Reliability	Availability	The fraction of time that a system is operative and accessible to its users
	Integrity	The probability that a system will not be compromised such as to perform incorrectly or return incorrect results
	Security	The probability that a system will not be compromised via access by unauthorized users
Usability	Ease of learning	The average amount of time required for a user to achieve a specified level of proficiency in using the system
	Ease of use	The average amount of time required for a proficient user to perform specified operations using the system
	Symmetry	The degree to which different parts of a system appear to the user to operate in a similar manner
Administrability	Configurability	The degree to which the program can be customized by the users to match their specific needs or preferences
	Installability	The amount of time required to install and initially configure the system

Table 5.3   Low-Level Quality Attribute Mapping (continued)

Standard Attributes	Lower-Level Attributes	Description
Maintainability	Expandability	The average amount of time required to add or remove a stated amount of functionality (e.g., one stimulus–response) to or from the system
	Portability	The average amount of time required to make the system operable on a different platform or in a different or modified environment
	Repairability	The average amount of time required to fix a bug in the system
Execution speed	Download speed	Speed in excess of capability requirements to transfer the program and its data over a network
	Launch speed	Speed in excess of capability requirements from the command to execute to the time the program is ready to accept user stimuli
	Run speed	Speed in excess of capability requirements for the program to respond to stimuli
Storage Demand	Mass storage demand	Persistent storage demand less than that specified by the capability requirements
	Memory demand	Program execution memory demand less than that specified by the capability requirements

Is required functionality the reason for developing the inventory system?

The team decides it is. The purpose of the inventory system is to provide up-to-date product information to the order processing and marketing departments. Functionality remains the #1 ranked quality attribute.

5.6.2 Reliability

Default ranked #2 because if a system is unreliable or unavailable it may not be able to perform its intended function when needed.

How important is timely availability and integrity of product information?

Marketing can tolerate short delays in information availability when creating a new catalogue, but publishing inaccurate information can lead to problems for the customer service staff. Order processing can tolerate no delay, regardless of whether the customer is on the phone or the Web site, because the result could be a lost sale. Furmasco has always claimed the customer is #1, so the team decides reliability must remain #2 to better support the customer.

5.6.3 Usability

Default ranked #3 because a program that is hard to use may preclude users from taking full advantage of its functionality, may adversely affect user productivity, or may even be actively avoided by users.

How important is ease of use to the human users of the inventory system, that is, the shipping and IT staff?

Coincidentally, the development team, being shipping and IT staff, are also among the future human users. There is no one who will suffer more from usability problems than they. The team immediately sees their vested self-interest in this quality attribute, and know they will do an adequate job on usability based on their own preferences, regardless of the rankings. Thus, they make a conscious decision to rank other quality attributes, such as maintainability, over usability to ensure these other attributes receive proper attention. They decide to move usability from #3 to #4.

5.6.4 Administerability

Default ranked #4 because a program that is difficult to install or administer may result in a system administrator not being able to install or configure it properly, thereby compromising some of its functionality, or perhaps making the program unavailable for use at all.

How important is administerability to the IT staff who will install and administer the inventory system?

As in the case of usability, the IT staff on the development team see their vested self-interest in this quality attribute. They decide to reduce its ranking for similar reasons. Because administration of the inventory system is expected to be less frequent, and therefore less costly, than daily usage, they decide to rank administerability below usability. Administerability is moved from #4 to #5.

5.6.5 Maintainability

Default ranked #5 because the labor cost of maintenance is generally higher than the hardware cost of speed or storage, but is generally less significant than the economics of day-to-day usage inherent in reliability and usability.

How important is expandability, portability, and repairability of the inventory system?

The team recalls the discussion with management, who indicated that, if the cost of maintaining in-house code appears high, they should buy one of the proprietary off-the-shelf inventory systems. Shipping, recalling old battles with the vendor of the current inventory system, wants control of the inventory system that only in-house development can provide. In their view, after functionality and reliable support of the customers, maintainability is paramount as it lies on the path to full control of their system. Cognizant of the challenges of software maintenance, the team members from IT are less enthusiastic about developing the inventory system in-house, but agree that maintainability deserves to be ranked #3 instead of #5 in this case.

5.6.6 Execution Speed

Default ranked #6 because of the continually decreasing cost of machine cycles. However, more speed can translate to improved economics of use, making speed more important than storage demand.

How important is execution speed in excess of stated capability requirements?

The team is unanimous that speed in excess of explicitly stated performance requirements does not have higher priority than the previous quality attributes. They decide to keep execution speed ranked at #6.

5.6.7 Storage Demand

Default ranked #7 because of the continually decreasing cost of storage, including both volatile (e.g., RAM) and persistent (e.g., disk or tape) storage.

How important is reduced storage demand in excess of stated capability requirements for storage?

The team sees no reason to alter this ranking as well. They retain the default storage demand ranking of #7.

Thus, after careful analysis of the issues surrounding each quality attribute, the development team publishes the quality requirements for the inventory system. Members of the team are each handed a sheet of paper to post at their workstations to remind them of the evaluation criteria to use when making even the smallest development decision. On this piece of paper is printed Table 5.4.

Table 5.4 Inventory System Quality Requirements

Rank	Quality Attribute	Rationale for Ranking
1	Functionality	Purpose of system is to provide up-to-date product information to order processing and marketing
2	Reliability	Customer service and "making the sale" require fast and accurate product information
3	Maintainability	In-house development and control of the system hinges on lowering the cost of maintenance
4	Usability	Because the developers are also the users, they instinctively will meet their usability expectations
5	Administerability	Because the developers will also install and configure the system, they will instinctively ensure admin effort is low
6	Execution speed	Speed in excess of stated capability requirements is not important
7	Storage demand	Storage reduction in excess of stated capability requirements is not important

References

1. Fox, A. and Patterson, D. 2003. Self-repairing computers. *Scientific American* (June), 54–58.

Chapter 6

Stimulus Identification and Cohesion

6.1 Chapter Overview

With the quality requirements specified, work can begin on the capability requirements. Capability requirements identify required functionality in terms of the external interface of the software. As advocated by Harlan Mills, a stimulus–response paradigm is used to specify required behavior.[1] The first step in specifying requirements using a stimulus–response paradigm is to identify all external stimuli detectable by the software system. This chapter explores the elements of stimulus identification, including types of stimuli and criteria that cohere stimuli into groups called "stimulus sets."

The protocols used to express the stimulus–response behavior, being externally visible information as well, are also specified as part of the capability requirements. These protocols include the look and feel of the human user interface, and communication protocols to external systems and the environment. This chapter introduces techniques for recording these protocols in rough form for purposes of stimulus identification.

The role of stimulus identification in the Freedom requirements process is illustrated in Figure 6.1, in which the topics of this chapter are identified by shaded boxes. The shading illustrates that specification of the human interface and communication protocols play a role in stimulus identification.

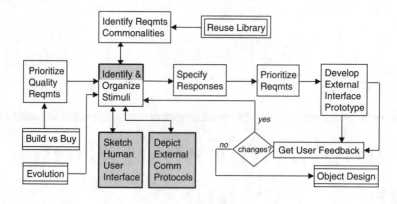

Figure 6.1   Stimulus identification in the requirements process.

6.2 What Is a Stimulus?

The dictionary defines a stimulus as "anything that causes a response." Because requirements in Freedom are software black box centric, Freedom defines stimuli in terms of the software black box. A stimulus is a message or signal detectable by the system black box.

6.2.1 Types of Stimuli

There are two types of stimuli: data stimuli and command stimuli.

Data stimuli are values with semantic meaning to the problem being solved by the program. Examples include (but are not limited to) data typed into data entry fields or onto command lines by users, data read from files or data bases, and data received over a network connection. The data may be saved, transmitted, used in a computation, or used in any way or purpose necessary and consistent with its semantic value to the problem being solved.

Command stimuli are trigger values that have no semantic meaning to the problem being solved by the program. The simplest and most common example is the value created by a button when pressed by a user. The value has no intrinsic semantics to the problem being solved; it merely acts as a signal to initiate some response.

Another example is an XML tag value, such as "name" in the XML fragment

```
<name>Rick</name>
```

"name" has no intrinsic value to the problem being solved. We could just as easily change "name" to "xxx" in the XML document type definition (DTD) and it would make no effective difference. Thus, "name" is a command stimulus. However, the value "Rick" is a data stimulus; it cannot arbitrarily be changed to, say, "Pete" without some significant change in the results of the program; for example, Pete may (erroneously) go to jail instead of Rick if, say, the XML file is a list of convicted felons.

This example also demonstrates a common relationship among the types of stimuli: command stimuli often act as delimiters for data stimuli. This is particularly common in streaming input from sources such as formatted files (of which XML is but a special case).

Which takes us back to input. When most people use the term "input," they are usually thinking in terms of data: that is, "input" and "input data" are essentially synonymous in most people's minds. Conversely, most people do not usually associate the term "input" with a button press (except, perhaps, developers who write lots of GUI (Graphical User Interface) code). Hence, a stimulus is almost the same as input data, with one difference:

```
input == data
stimulus == command or data
```

Thus, Freedom uses the term "stimuli" in lieu of "input" to help ensure that command stimuli are not ignored or forgotten.

6.2.2 Sources of Stimuli

As an aid to stimulus identification, it is useful to consider stimuli as consisting of three types based on their source, as illustrated in Figure 6.2: human user stimuli, external system stimuli, and environment stimuli.

Human user stimuli consist of commands and data originating from human users of the system. Human command stimuli are input events that simply request a response, such as a button press. Human data stimuli are input data values that may be stored internally by the system or used in some calculation or other algorithm. Various input mechanisms may be used to provide human user stimuli such as graphical user interfaces, command line interfaces, hardware control panels, voice, and tactile (touch-sensitive pads). Experiments with monkeys have successfully demonstrated computer control directly from brain waves, so who knows what form human user interfaces of the future may take! Fortunately for purposes of stimulus identification, the exact mechanism to be used is irrelevant. Only the fact that the system must detect a particular command or data stimulus is relevant to stimulus identification.

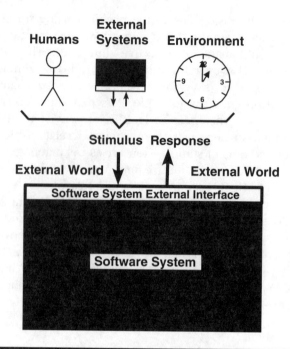

Figure 6.2   Sources of stimuli.

External system stimuli are message commands and data sent by a system external to the system being built. The message stream may be sent using any mechanism—wire (network, TV cable, tugs on a string) or wireless (satellite, RF, microwave, smoke signals)—the mechanism used is irrelevant to stimulus identification. The message may originate from any type of external system—software or hardware, local or remote—the details of the sending system are also irrelevant (i.e., the external system is a black box too). Only the fact that the system must detect a particular command or data stimulus is relevant to stimulus identification.

Environment stimuli are signals originating from the physical environment, typically from sensors. Environment data stimuli are detected via sensors such as thermometers, pressure gauges, radar, or clocks. Time is perhaps the most common type of environment stimulus as software often needs to be sensitive to time for proper operation. Environment command stimuli are usually detected via binary sensors, for example, two-state switches, in which, for example, "on" is a stimulus and "off" is no stimulus. Although the type of environment stimulus (command or data) is likely to be of importance, the exact nature of its source (i.e., the implementation details of the sensor) is irrelevant. Only the fact that the system must detect a particular command or data stimulus is relevant to stimulus identification.

The above classification of stimuli into three groups may result in ambiguity in some cases. For example, a radioactive particle count may be categorized as an environment stimulus because the radiation originates from an object in the environment. However, some may argue it is an external system stimulus because an external system, say a Geiger counter, is the direct source of the signal detected by the software. In such cases, it is less important how the stimulus is categorized, and more important that the requirements identify the particular signal or quantity as a relevant stimulus. Categorization of stimuli into three categories is fundamentally just an aid to stimulus identification. The most important thing is not to miss a relevant stimulus.

A given application may not need to detect stimuli from all the above sources. For example, desktop applications may have human user interfaces only. Embedded applications may have external system interfaces only. Other applications, such as aircraft flight control systems, may have all three types of interface. In general, an external interface may contain any or all of the three sources of stimuli:

```
external interface == human stimuli + external system
    stimuli + environment stimuli
```

6.3 Stimulus Sets

Because the number of stimuli detectable by a system may be large, an effective complexity management technique is needed to help people deal with the the complexity. Freedom uses two organizational strategies for this purpose. The first is to collect stimuli into sets based on cohesion. The second is to organize the sets into a treelike structure called a "functionality tree." Functionality trees are covered in a subsequent chapter. Here, we consider grouping of stimuli into sets based on their cohesion.

A single cohesive collection of stimuli is called a "stimulus set." There are at least eight commonly recognized types of cohesion,[2] however, it is generally sufficient to consider only three when grouping stimuli into sets: functional, physical,[3] and temporal cohesion.

Stimuli have functional cohesion when they relate to the same task, operation, or object. For example, the data stimuli "user name" and "password" have functional cohesion because they are both components of a log-in function.

Stimuli are physically cohesive when they are physically or spatially co-located in the system interface. For example, the data components of a log-in function might all be physically located in the same pop-up window or otherwise grouped together.

Table 6.1   Stimulus Set Cohesion

Cohesion Type	Description
Functional	**Stimuli relate to the same task, operation, or object**
Physical	**Stimuli are physically or spatially co-located**
Informational	Series of independent actions on a datum
Sequential	Output from one function is input to next, e.g., pipeline
Communicational	A sequence of steps on the same data
Procedural	A sequence of steps
Temporal	**Stimuli are or can be active at the same time**
Logical	Series of actions related by externally selected parameters
Coincidental	Series of unrelated actions or module elements

Stimuli are temporally cohesive when they are, or can be, active at the same time. For example, the data components of a log-in function might all be active and able to accept input from the user at the same time.

Just how cohesive are stimulus sets? The cohesive strength of a software entity, such as a module or function, is determined by the kind of cohesion exhibited. Table 6.1 lists the common types of cohesion in order of decreasing strength, with functional cohesion being the strongest and coincidental the weakest. The three types of stimuli that bond stimuli into stimulus sets are identified by the three bold entries in the table. Most software entities exhibit only one type of cohesion. Stimulus sets exhibit three, including two of the strongest. It should be evident from the table that stimulus sets are among the most cohesive of all software entities.

One might think that achieving such high levels of cohesion in stimulus sets involves much work. Not true. Creating stimulus sets with triple-high levels of cohesion is easy because such cohesion occurs naturally in external interfaces. Some examples illustrate this point.

6.3.1 Example Human User Stimulus Set

Stimulus sets occur in a natural and obvious way in human user interfaces. They also occur in communication streams to external systems and the environment, although this is not quite as obvious due to the "invisible" nature of programmatic streams. Thus, it is easier to learn about stimulus sets using a human user interface as an example.

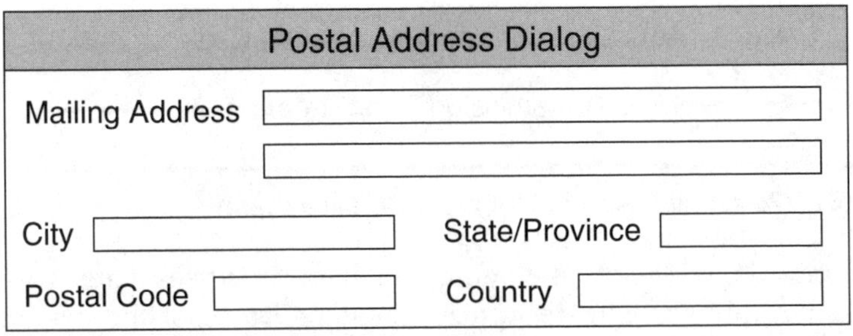

Figure 6.3   Postal address stimulus set, human user.

The current state of the practice is to implement human user interfaces using graphical technologies. When graphical interfaces are used, a human user stimulus set will usually take the form of a window, menu bar, dialog box, pop-up menu, or similar "container" component. An example of a human user stimulus set is the hypothetical postal address dialog box shown in Figure 6.3. This stimulus set contains five stimuli in the form of data entry fields that allow the user to enter the various parts of a postal address. The five stimuli are part of the same stimulus set because they have all three types of cohesion. The five fields are functionally cohesive because they all deal with the same kind of object, namely, a postal address. They are physically cohesive because they are co-located in the same dialog window. They are temporally cohesive because the entry fields are all able to accept user input at the same time.

A rule of thumb to keep in mind for human user stimuli is not to group too many stimuli into one stimulus set. Studies have shown that human perception becomes less focused or more confused when the number of combinatorial choices presented at one time exceeds a limit roughly expressed as "7 ± 2." This human factors guideline postulated by Miller[4] indicates that the number of stimuli in a human user stimulus set should not exceed nine. For groups of stimuli with conceptually complex interactions that require more thought, Warfield[5] suggested the number should not exceed three:

> There is evidence that much of what goes on in society is defective because of the failure of human beings to comprehend the limitations on human thought processes. . . .

> By joining the findings of psychology with certain specialized findings from mathematics, it is possible to use information structures that on one hand permit open assessment of cognitive limits, and on the other give form and substance to complex packages of information. . . .

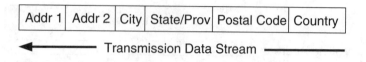

Figure 6.4   Postal address stimulus set, external system.

> A critical guideline in the improvement of processes that involve human thought is to recognize the significance of the magical number three, plus or minus zero.

On the other hand, familiar choice sets such as an alphabetized list of the 50 states can safely exceed the theoretical cognitive limits inasmuch as familiarity with the subject matter, and lack of any interaction between the choices, is sufficient to avoid cognitive overload and confusion.

6.3.2 Example External-System Stimulus Set

The same principle of functional, physical, and temporal cohesion used to group human user stimuli into stimulus sets also applies to external system and environment stimuli.

Consider the case of an external system that sends stimuli to the system being built in the form of a network data stream, such as shown in Figure 6.4. In this case, each data record in the transmission protocol would be a stimulus set and each constituent data value would be a stimulus. The data are functionally cohesive as they all relate to the object or operation underlying the record. The data are physically and temporally cohesive as they are co-located in the same record, and transmitted at the same time in the same communication stream.

From the standpoint of protocol, stimulus sets originating in the environment are similar in nature to stimulus sets originating from external software systems. In some cases, the distinction is largely academic.

It should be mentioned that the "7 ± 2" human factors rule of thumb is less relevant for external system and environment stimuli because the computer does not have the same cognitive limits that a human mind does. However, humans have to maintain the software that implements these stimulus sets and, therefore, the number of stimuli in external system and environment stimulus sets should be kept within reasonable limits to promote ease of maintenance.

6.3.3 Source-Neutral Stimulus Set Recording

Freedom uses a simple listlike textual notation for recording stimulus sets in a source-neutral manner. The notation consists of the name of the

Listing 6.1   Postal Address Stimulus Set, Source Neutral

```
SS Postal Address
Mailing Address 1
Mailing Address 2
City
State/Province
Postal Code
Country
```

stimulus set above a list of names of the constituent stimuli. When recorded using the Freedom source-neutral stimulus set notation, the example postal address stimulus set appears as shown in Listing 6.1. This notation records only the essential information of the stimulus set, that is, its name and the names of its constituent stimuli. Hence, it is completely independent of the mechanism or technology that will be used to implement the stimuli, such as graphical or network technology, and is therefore independent of the source of the stimuli. When recorded using source-neutral notation, the example human user and external system postal address stimulus sets appear identical.

6.4 Functionality Screens

For several reasons, the human user part of the external interface deserves special attention. First, it is the part of the external interface directly visible to the customer; its look and feel must be acceptable to the user. Some users may even insist on seeing up front what the human user interface will look like. External system and environment interfaces are not as subject to user scrutiny. Second, the human user interface must take human factors considerations into account. Third, because developers are users too, most are very familiar with human user interfaces and are therefore more adept at identifying needed stimuli when presented in the form of a human interface.

A notation for giving the user an early look at the human user interface, while leveraging the developer's familiarity with human interfaces to aid in stimulus identification, is called a "functionality screen." A functionality screen is a sketch or rough depiction of a human user interface. It does not strive to be the finished or final look and feel, but is simply a best guess at the start of the project. Any responsive means may be used to draw the functionality screens, such as general-purpose computer drawing tools, "keyboard art," or even pencil and paper (the author uses the backs of old business cards). One functionality screen is drawn for each screen or window, each of which may contain one or more stimulus sets.

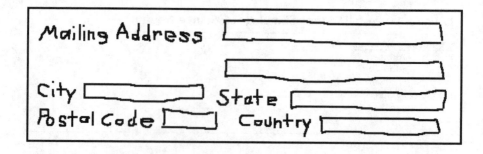

Figure 6.5   Postal address functionality screen, sketch.

Listing 6.2   Postal Address Functionality Screen, Keyboard Art

```
Mailing Address  |_____|

                 |_____|
City  |_____|   State/Province |_____|

Postal Code   |_____|   Country   |_____|
```

Figure 6.5 shows a functionality screen for the postal address dialog window. This functionality screen represents a sketch such as might be drawn with pencil and paper. Sketches are good for functionality screens because they are fast and easy to draw, and require no special tools. In fact, they do not even require a computer, and so can be created during team meetings or even during lunch with the customer.

Listing 6.2 is another functionality screen for the same postal address dialog window. This variant was drawn with keyboard art, that is, using only the characters on a standard ASCII keyboard. Keyboard art takes a little longer to create than pencil and paper sketches, but are neater and perhaps easier to modify. They also have the big advantage of being able to be included as comments in the code that implements the look and feel of the human user interface. The author regularly includes keyboard art functionality screens in the implementing code. This is a good way to document the purpose of the code without a lot of words ("a picture is worth a thousand words") and is a great way to get amazed looks from other developers, especially those who have not yet developed a full appreciation for the benefits of code comments.

Regardless of their utility for purposes such as giving the users an early look at the proposed human interface, and commenting the implementing code, the primary purpose of functionality screens is to help identify human user stimuli.

6.5 Programmatic Protocols

A programmatic protocol is a data stream passed between two system black boxes. Because it is external to both systems, a programmatic protocol is requirements information for the participating systems.

There are limitless possible formats for programmatic protocols. In an attempt to instill a measure of regularity, interoperability, and cost control, a number of standard programmatic protocols have been defined. Examples include TCP/IP for network data transmission, and XML for semantic tagging of data. Protocols are often layered. TCP/IP is actually a layered set of seven protocols. Standard protocols are often carriers for application-specific protocols. For example, XML and custom protocols are often layered above TCP/IP.

Standard protocols are usually supported by reusable software packages, and sometimes hardware. Thus, the details of a standard protocol need not be specified in a requirements specification when the application is to use an available package for the protocol. However, if the program is to use an application-specific protocol, then the details of that protocol should be defined as part of the requirements, starting with identification of stimuli and stimulus sets for the protocol.

Although an application-specific protocol may be any format, a very common, simple, yet effective format is the "command-data" stream.

6.5.1 Command-Data Streams

A command-data stream is a generic format for an application-specific protocol. Command-data streams are structured as a series of command-data pairs, as follows.

```
< command >< data values >
     :             :
< command >< data values >
```

The command is a short value or string that identifies the type of data that follows. When the protocol is being defined, the exact value chosen for a command is arbitrary. Once a command value has been selected, however, it cannot ever be changed. If it were, existing data files that use the custom protocol would instantly be rendered obsolete, and perhaps unreadable.

Zero or more data values are associated with each command value. The data values may be numbers, characters, binary, or any other type or combination of types. The exact types and sequence of the data values, if any, following the command depends on the command.

Listing 6.3   Postal Address Command-Data Read Protocol

```
30            -- level 1 cmd (postal address)
31            -- level 2 cmd (address)
address 1     -- level 3 data
address 2     -- level 3 data
32            -- level 2 cmd (city)
city          -- level 3 data
33            -- level 2 cmd (state/providence)
state/prov    -- level 3 data
34            -- level 2 cmd (postal code)
postal_code   -- level 3 data
35            -- level 2 cmd (country)
country       -- level 3 data
39            -- level 2 cmd (end postal address)
```

Command-data streams are efficient. Very little transmission bandwidth is wasted on protocol overhead. Also, command-data streams are relatively easy to parse.

Command-data streams usually contain no provision for error recovery of dropped or altered bits. This is often because they are embedded within one or more standard carrier protocols, and one of the carrier protocols provides the error correction.

Command-data streams are not intended to be human readable. Human readability is relinquished in favor of transmission and processing efficiency. Hence, command-data streams are usually transmitted in binary.

Even if they were transmitted in plaintext form, the semantics of command-data streams may not be obvious because the semantics of the values in the stream are defined in external documents and, especially, in the software that reads and writes the streams. In some cases the lack of obvious semantics can be an advantage, such as when security is a concern. Third parties that do not have access to the application-specific parsing code cannot easily decode the streams.

When recording the requirements for a programmatic protocol such as a command-data stream, each command and datum in the stream represents a stimulus. Like all other stimuli, they can be organized into stimulus sets based on cohesion. That is, interfaces to external systems and the environment are treated exactly the same as interfaces to human users. Some examples serve to illustrate this point.

Listing 6.3 is a custom command-data stream for the programmatic version of the postal address stimulus set shown in Figure 6.4. In this example, each command-data pair is split into two lines with the command on the first line followed by the associated data on the second. The example also uses a two-tier command structure, with some commands simply triggering a shift to the next lower or higher logical level of the command structure.

The first command-data pair consists of the high-level command stimulus 30, which signifies a shift to the next lowest level of the command structure. There is no associated data value; that is, the "pair" is really a singleton command.

The second command-data pair starts with the Level 2 command stimulus 31, which signifies that an address string follows on the next line. The address string is a data stimulus.

The third command-data pair starts with the Level 2 command 32, which signifies that a data stimulus representing the city follows.

The fourth command-data pair starts with the Level 2 command 33, which signifies that a data stimulus representing the state or province follows. Likewise, the fifth pair is the command stimulus 34 followed by the data stimulus for the postal or zip code, and the sixth pair is the command stimulus 35 followed by the data stimulus for the country name.

The final command-data pair is the Level 2 command 39, which causes a logical shift back to the upper level of the command structure. Like command 30, command 39 is a singleton command with no associated data value.

The stimuli for any command-data stream can be grouped into stimulus sets. Doing so is a straightforward two-step process.

Step 1: Group Command Stimuli by Level

Command stimuli that are at the same level cohere into the same stimulus set. Such stimuli are functionally cohesive due to being commands, physically cohesive due to being at the same logical level, and temporally cohesive due to being valid for detection or parsing at the same time. Commands that are logically at lower levels, if any, group into lower-level stimulus sets based both on level and detectability (temporal cohesion).

The example command-data stream in Listing 6.3 contains commands at two levels. All the commands at Level 1, namely 30, cohere into one stimulus set. The Level 2 commands that are active at the same time group into additional stimulus sets. "Active at the same time" means that a parser will recognize the value as a command, and not a "bad value," at that point in the parsing. In the example protocol, all Level 2 stimuli, 31 through 39, are active at the same time so they all group into one stimulus set. As a result, two stimulus sets represent the commands in the postal address example. These stimulus sets (SS) appear in Listing 6.4 as Record Type SS and Postal Addr Field SS.

Step 2: Group Data Stimuli by Command

For the data in a command-data protocol, create a stimulus set for each unique dataset associated with each type of command.

Listing 6.4   Postal Address Command-Data Read Stimulus Sets

Record Type SS	Postal Addr Field SS	Mail Addr SS
30	31	address 1
	32	address 2
	33	
	34	
	35	
	39	

City SS	State SS	Postal Code SS	Country SS
city	state	zip	country

In the postal address example, five commands, 31 through 35, have associated datasets. For command 31, the dataset consists of two address strings (for handling multi-line street addresses). These strings form one stimulus set. For commands 32 through 35, the associated dataset contains one string. Each of these data strings forms a separate stimulus set for data. The result is the five data stimulus sets labeled Mail Addr SS, City SS, State SS, Postal Code SS, and Country SS shown in Listing 6.4.

6.5.2 XML Streams

An XML stream is a standard format for semantic tagging and communication of data within a given discipline. The full details of XML are given by Bray,[6] but the basic idea is to associate semantics with data via "elements" of the form:

```
<tag_name  attribute_name="attribute_value">
   data_string </tag_name>
```

The element begins with <tag_name>, which is a string that identifies the type of data that follows. The attribute name-value pairs define information of interest to the application that will process the data, for example, the color in which to display the data. The data_string may define an actual datum, or may be another tag_name-data element; thus, elements may be nested. The </tag_name> (begins with "</") string ends the element.

XML-formatted data is human readable and semantically clear, at least relatively speaking. Most important, the tag_names and attribute_names are standardized for a given discipline or industry, permitting interoperability of data files and programmatic streams.

These benefits, especially interoperability, are important but are purchased at the price of efficiency. XML protocol overhead can be a factor of 10 or more (10 or more overhead bits to one data bit) compared to binary command-data streams. Also, complete XML streams are much more complex than shown above, and so are complex to parse. Fortunately,

Listing 6.5   Postal Address XML Protocol

```
<postal_addr>
    <mail_addr>address 1,
               address 2</mail_addr>
    <city>city</city>
    <state>state</state>
    <postal_code>zip</postal_code>
    <country>country</country>
</postal_addr>
```

standard parses for XML are available. This eliminates the need for most applications to deal with the full details of XML, allowing them to focus instead on the tags and attributes.

Listing 6.5 is an example XML stream for the programmatic version of the postal address stimulus set shown in Figure 6.4. This XML example uses a two-level element structure, with five lower-level elements (mail_addr, city, state, postal_code, country) nested within one upper-level element (postal_addr).

Like any other programmatic protocol, XML streams can be organized into stimulus sets based on cohesion. The <tag_name> that begins an element is a command stimulus, and each data_string is a data stimulus. Each </tag_name> that ends an element, although technically a command stimulus, is treated as a data stimulus due to temporal cohesion; that is, it is detectable at the same time as the data_string of the element. The result is a straightforward and, by now, familiar two-step process, illustrated below using the same postal address example for comparison.

Step 1: Group Command Stimuli by Level

Command stimuli (i.e., XML <tag_name> declarations) that are at the same level and detectable at the same time cohere into the same stimulus set. Such stimuli are functionally cohesive due to being commands, physically cohesive due to being at the same logical level, and temporally cohesive due to being valid for detection or parsing at the same time. Commands (i.e., XML <tag_name> declarations) that are logically at lower levels also group into lower-level stimulus sets based both on level and detectability (temporal cohesion).

The example XML stream in Listing 6.5 contains <tag_name> commands at two levels. All the commands at Level 1, namely, <postal_addr>, cohere into one stimulus set. The Level 2 commands that are active at the same time group into additional stimulus sets. In the example protocol, all Level 2 command stimuli, <mail_addr> through <country> plus the </postal_addr> element terminator, are active at the same time so they all group into one stimulus set. As a result, two stimulus sets represent the commands in the

Listing 6.6   Postal Address XML Stimulus Sets

Record Type SS	Postal Addr Field SS	Mail Addr SS
<postal_addr>	<mail_addr>	address 1
	<city>	address 2
	<state>	</mail_addr>
	<postal_code>	
	<country>	
	</postal_addr>	

City SS	State SS	Postal Code SS	Country SS
city	state	zip	country
</city>	</state>	</postal_code>	</country>

postal address example. These stimulus sets appear in Listing 6.6 as Record Type SS and Postal Addr Field SS.

Step 2: Group Data Stimuli by Command

For the data in XML elements, create a stimulus set for each unique set of data stimuli associated with each type of <tag_name> command stimulus.

In the postal address example, five commands stimuli, <mail_addr> through <country>, have associated data stimuli. For <mail_addr>, the data consist of two address strings (for handling multi-line street addresses). These strings form one stimulus set. For <city> through <country>, the associated datasets contain one data stimulus string each. Each of these data strings forms a separate stimulus set for data. The result is the five stimulus sets labeled Mail Addr SS, City SS, State SS, Postal Code SS, and Country SS shown in Listing 6.6.

Note that the two-step process and the resulting example stimulus sets are nearly identical for both command-data and XML protocols. Stimulus set analysis tends to wash out implementation differences, promoting a focus on stimulus identification. Preliminary definition of specific protocols for human and programmatic interfaces can thus aid in stimulus identification without the protocol details becoming an undue distraction from the primary goal.

6.6 Example Problem Functionality Screen

With the quality requirements for the Furmasco furniture inventory system specified, the shipping department development team begins specification of the capability requirements. They decide to identify stimuli for the human user interface first, due to their familiarity with human interfaces.

Listing 6.7   Inventory System Functionality Screen

```
-----------------------------------------------------------------------
|                   Furmasco Furniture Inventory            Quit |
|---------------------------------------------------------------------|
|     Furniture Classification        |        List of Furniture      |
|                                     |                             _|
|      --------------------           | xxx xxxxxxxxxxxxxxxxxxxxxxx  |^|
|     | <classif categ> |^|           | xxx xxxxxxxxxxxxxxxxxxxxxxx  |_|
|      --------------------           | xxx xxxxxxxxxxxxxxxxxxxxxxx  |-|
|      --------------------           | xxx xxxxxxxxxxxxxxxxxxxxxxx  | |
|     | Select Type     |^|           | xxx xxxxxxxxxxxxxxxxxxxxxxx  | |
|      --------------------           | xxx xxxxxxxxxxxxxxxxxxxxxxx  | |
|-------------------------------------| xxx xxxxxxxxxxxxxxxxxxxxxxx  | |
|         Furniture Data              | xxx xxxxxxxxxxxxxxxxxxxxxxx  | |
|                  _____       | xxx xxxxxxxxxxxxxxxxxxxxxxx  | |
|      Descrip   |_____|  |     | xxx xxxxxxxxxxxxxxxxxxxxxxx  | |
|                  _____            | xxx xxxxxxxxxxxxxxxxxxxxxxx  | |
|     Quantity   |_____|           | xxx xxxxxxxxxxxxxxxxxxxxxxx  | |
|                  _____            | xxx xxxxxxxxxxxxxxxxxxxxxxx  | |
|        Price   |_____|           | xxx xxxxxxxxxxxxxxxxxxxxxxx  | |
|                  _____            | xxx xxxxxxxxxxxxxxxxxxxxxxx  | |
|      Ship Wt   |_____|           | xxx xxxxxxxxxxxxxxxxxxxxxxx  | |
|                  _____         | xxx xxxxxxxxxxxxxxxxxxxxxxx  | |
|    Dimensions  |_w,_h,_d___|        | xxx xxxxxxxxxxxxxxxxxxxxxxx  | |
|       _____       _____        | xxx xxxxxxxxxxxxxxxxxxxxxxx  | |
|      | Select |     | Reset |       | xxx xxxxxxxxxxxxxxxxxxxxxxx  | |
|       ----------     ---------       | xxx xxxxxxxxxxxxxxxxxxxxxxx  |v|
|-------------------------------------------------------------------|
|               <x> View    < > Add    < > Modify                   |
|-------------------------------------------------------------------|
| message area                                                      |
 -------------------------------------------------------------------
```

As a first step to identifying human user stimuli, they develop a functionality screen in consultation with users of the existing inventory system. The resulting pencil sketch incorporates both functionality and usability improvements that are intended to fix long-standing problems with the graphical interface of the current proprietary inventory system. The functionality screen sketch is redrawn by one of the team members from IT using keyboard art for later inclusion in the code. The keyboard art version appears in Listing 6.7.

With the functionality screen (FS) defined, it is an easy matter to identify the stimulus sets based on physical co-location of stimuli in the FS. A quick check also reveals the co-located stimuli have functional and temporal cohesion, which not only validates the stimulus sets but also serves as a "sanity check" on the layout of the FS. Five stimulus sets (SS)—called Classification SS, Furniture List SS, Furniture Data SS, Mode SS, and Inventory SS—are identified as shown in Listing 6.8.

**Listing 6.8   Inventory System Human
User Stimulus Sets**

Classification SS	Furniture List SS
list of categories	list of furniture
list of types	
Furniture Data SS	**Main Operation SS**
description	view
quantity	add
price	modify
shipping weight	
dimensions (w,h,d)	**Inventory SS**
select	quit
reset	

6.7 Example Problem Programmatic Protocol

After identifying the human user stimuli, the team tackles the external system stimuli. As the context diagram shows, the inventory system must provide a programmatic query interface for use by the app server. As in the case of the human user interface, defining a preliminary protocol to the app server can result in easy identification of the needed programmatic stimuli and stimulus sets. What protocol should be used by the interface to the app server?

The team immediately starts discussing SQL. Eventually, someone points out that SQL, although an obvious protocol to the database, need not be the protocol to the app server. In fact, it might be best not to base communication with the app server on a protocol specific to relational databases; the fewer implementation details revealed in the app server interface, the better. After all, that is what a "black box view" means. Someone then suggests an XML-based protocol: "Everyone is using XML nowadays." Someone else suggests a command-data protocol: "It's more efficient than XML."

"Who cares? The communication will be over our high-speed LAN. Efficiency is not a problem. Standardization is more important."

"There is no XML standard for furniture inventory, or for any type of inventory system. XML is a metadata standard. What does it do for an inventory application? It just slows it down, that's what!"

The discussion starts to get heated, and the sides—just about everyone on the team has taken sides by now—seem to be drifting apart rather

Table 6.2   Inventory System Programmatic Protocol Trade-Off

Rank	Quality Attribute	Command-Data Stream	XML Stream
1	Functionality	Adequate: can do job	Adequate: can do job
2	Reliability	Adequate: shorter binary stream, no error checking	Adequate: longer text stream, no error checking
3	Maintainability	**Better: less complex implementing code**	Poor: more complex implementing code
4	Usability	Poor: less interoperable	**Excellent: more interoperable**
5	Administerability	**Good: no special needs**	Fair: must maintain DTD on network
6	Execution speed	**Good: more efficient**	Poor: less efficient
7	Storage demand	**Good: less bandwidth**	Poor: more bandwidth

than reaching consensus. Finally, someone sees the sheet of paper with the quality requirements posted next to the whiteboard.

"Let's see what the quality requirements say is best, XML or command-data streams."

The heated discussion abruptly stops. After a water-cooler break, a focused evaluation of the merits of XML versus command-data streams relative to each quality attribute ensues. Shortly, the team produces the trade-off comparison shown in Table 6.2.

With respect to functionality and reliability, the two alternatives are about equal. Both can provide the needed communication protocol, and reliability is not expected to be significantly different. The major differences are in maintainability and usability. The relative simplicity of command-data streams should make the implementing code easier to maintain, and tag format standardization should make XML more interoperable and usable across multiple domain applications. The standard quality attributes rank usability over maintainability, thus favoring XML. However, the quality attributes for the inventory system rank maintainability higher than usability, favoring command-data streams for this application. Although team members may argue with each other, there is no arguing with the quality requirements. Command-data streams are selected as the programmatic protocol.

Listing 6.9   Inventory System Programmatic Send Protocol

```
Inv Sys Inv Sys
Input   Output
01                         -- level 1 cmd (classif categ)
categ                      -- level 2 data (classif categ)
02                         -- level 1 cmd (classif type)
type                       -- level 2 data (classif type)
03      descrip list       -- level 1 cmd (description list)
10                         -- level 1 cmd (furniture data)
description                -- level 2 data (description)
12      quantity           -- level 3 cmd (quantity)
13      price              -- level 3 cmd (price)
14      shipping wt        -- level 3 cmd (shipping weight)
15      w,h,d              -- level 3 cmd (dimensions)
19                         -- level 3 cmd (end furn data)
```

Work then begins on specifying a preliminary command-data stream protocol for use by the app server. The context diagram shows the interface to the app server is read-only for the app server, or send-only for the inventory system. (All modifications and additions to the inventory will be via the human user interface.) This simplifies the programmatic protocol considerably. Discussions with the IT app server team indicate that dynamic Web page generation will require, first, the capability to display all furniture of a given classification type for a user to browse and, second, selective extraction of data for an item of a given description for a user to buy. Discussion leads to the three-level command-data protocol shown in Listing 6.9.

The inventory system will first listen for a Level 1 command 01, which is the signal that a classification category stimulus will follow. The inventory system then listens for a Level 2 "category" stimulus, such as "Living Room." When received, the inventory system goes back to listening for a Level 1 command. This sequence is repeated for the Level 1 command 02 for a classification type data stimulus, such as "Chairs." The inventory system now knows the type of furniture of interest to the app server user, such as "Living Room, Chairs." On receipt of the Level 1 command 03, the inventory system sends the app server a list of descriptions for all inventory items of the classification type of interest, for example, a list of descriptions for available models of "Living Room, Chairs." The app server user can now browse the available descriptions for that type of furniture. When he selects one of the descriptions, such as "Sofa Model 1234," the app server sends a Level 1 command 10, which is the signal that the selected description follows as a Level 2 stimulus. Receipt of the Level 2 description stimulus tells the inventory system that the item of interest is "Sofa Model 1234," and enables the Level 3 command stimuli 12 to 15. Receipt of one of these stimuli sends the specified datum for that stimulus

Listing 6.10   Inventory System Send Protocol Stimulus Sets

Cmd Type SS	Categ SS	Type SS	Furn Data SS
01	category	type	12
02			13
03			14
10			15
			19
Descrip SS			
description			

to the app server or, in the case of command stimulus 19, re-enables listening for Level 1 commands.

There is some discussion of adding a Level 3 command 16 to send a 3-D scene graph to the app server so the user can view the selected furniture item in 3-D using the CM Surveyor virtual reality browser, but the decision is made to include the virtual reality capability in the next release. The protocol can be easily expanded to include 3-D capability when the release 2 requirements are specified.

Identification of the programmatic stimuli and stimulus sets becomes easy once the preliminary protocol is defined. The team applies the two-step process: (1) group command stimuli by level, and (2) group data stimuli by command. The result for the inventory system command-data protocol is two command stimulus sets and three data stimulus sets, as shown in Listing 6.10.

The team lead dutifully notes that the time to define the programmatic protocol, identify the stimuli, and group them into stimulus sets was hardly more than the team spent in the ad hoc discussion over which type of protocol to use. That discussion could have gone on forever! She then realized that, for the immediate purposes of stimulus identification, the decision made little difference because similar stimulus sets would likely have resulted for either protocol. The quality requirements quickly and amicably settled an issue that was largely insignificant to the task at hand. Now, the project was actually ahead of schedule. Thank goodness for the quality requirements!

References

1. Mills, H. 1988. Stepwise refinement and verification in box-structured systems. *IEEE Computer*, 21: 6 (June).
2. Coupling and cohesion, Web page and wiki, 2004. Available at http://c2. com/cgi/wiki?CouplingAndCohesion.
3. Physical cohesion is not generally recognized as a kind of module or process cohesion in the literature, but is highly relevant to stimuli.

4. Miller, G. 1956. The magical number seven, plus or minus two: Some limits on our capacity for processing information. *Psychology Review* 63:2,

5. Warfield, P. 1987. The magical number three—Plus or minus zero. In *Annual Meeting of The International Society for General Systems Research*, Budapest, Hungary.

6. Bray, T. et al., editors 2004. *Extensible Markup Language (XML) 1.0* (Third Edition), W3C, Available at http://www.w3.org/TR/2004/REC-xml-20040204/.

Chapter 7

Stimulus Organization and Architecture

7.1 Chapter Overview

Freedom organizes stimuli in two ways: (1) by grouping stimuli into stimulus sets based on functional, physical, and temporal cohesion, and (2) arranging the stimulus sets into a hierarchy called a functionality tree. Stimulus set grouping was covered in Chapter 6. This chapter looks at functionality trees and the organization of stimulus sets into a treelike architecture.

The role of stimulus organization in the Freedom requirements process is illustrated in Figure 7.1. In the figure, the topic of this chapter is identified by box shading.

7.2 Stimulus Set Architecture

At the same time that stimuli are identified and grouped into stimulus sets, the stimulus sets are organized into a hierarchy called the "stimulus set architecture." It can just as accurately be called the "external interface architecture" because the stimuli are part of the external interface, or the "requirements architecture" because requirements are defined as the software system external interface. The external interface architecture works with the stimulus sets to manage external interface (i.e., requirements) complexity.

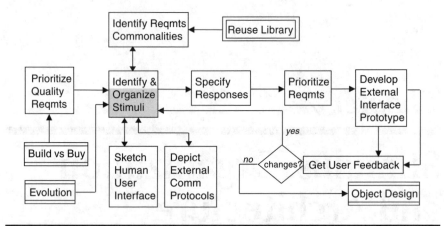

Figure 7.1 Stimulus organization in the requirements process.

The external interface architecture plays another role as well: it is the design of the requirements. The concept of requirements having a design may seem strange until one considers that requirements are defined as the software system external interface, and external interfaces certainly have a design. In the familiar case of a human user interface, the design includes the assignment of buttons and other interface components to menus and windows, that is, stimulus set cohesion. The design also consists of the hierarchical organization of menus and windows, that is, the external interface architecture.

The external interface architecture plays the same complexity management and design roles for interfaces to external systems and the environment as it does for human user interfaces. In fact, the notation that records the external interface architecture does not differentiate among different sources of stimuli, nor implementation protocol details. The external interface architecture recording notation is implementation neutral. It is called a functionality tree.

7.3 New Stimulus Response

One of the possible responses to a stimulus is to change the activation status of one or more stimuli. For example, consider a log-in screen. Entering a correct password (a stimulus) may cause the username and password entry fields (two stimuli) to be deactivated and cause a menu (a set of new stimuli) to be activated. Freedom calls this type of response a "New Stimulus Response" (NSR). The term is a bit of a misnomer because NSR encompasses deactivation of existing stimuli as well as activation of new stimuli.

7.4 Functionality Trees

A functionality tree is a "horizontal tree" notation for recording the external interface architecture. A functionality tree depicts a type of entity-relationship model where the entities are all stimulus sets, and the relationships are all New Stimulus Responses.

Syntactically, a functionality tree is a horizontal hierarchy with the hierarchical levels arranged in columns. Each column represents a "depth level," which is the hierarchical distance of the stimulus sets in that level from the "root" of the tree. The root consists of the stimulus sets in the leftmost column, designated as "Level 0" because they are zero distance from the root. Deeper stimulus sets are arranged in successive columns to the right with monotonically increasing level numbers. The "leaves" of the tree are the stimulus sets in the locally deepest rightmost columns. The local depth of the hierarchy may vary.

Semantically, the root, Level 0, stimulus sets (SS) are those that are displayed to the user or otherwise made active when the program is first started. Level 1 SSs are those that become active when triggered by detection of stimuli at Level 0. In general, a Level n SS becomes active in response (NSR) to a stimulus in a Level $n - 1$ SS.

Tools suitable for creation of functionality trees must be capable of maintaining proper column alignment. Commodity tools such as spreadsheets, and text editors that use fixed-pitch fonts, are adequate, and low cost or free. Thus, functionality trees can be developed quickly, easily, and inexpensively.

The number of functionality trees per application, that is, per software system black box, is exactly one. In some cases the functionality tree may become large, and printing or similar considerations may necessitate breaking the functionality tree into parts. This is acceptable. Any reasonable criteria may be used to define the break boundaries. Stimulus source, for example, breaks a tree into human, external system, and environment subtrees. When breaking a functionality tree, always remember that all subtrees are part of one, and only one, functionality tree for the system black box. Thus, all subtrees should fit cleanly together. If they do not, the partitioning is incorrect.

7.5 Sample Functionality Tree

An sample functionality tree is shown in Figure 7.2. As shown in the figure, a functionality tree may be drawn graphically or textually. When drawn graphically, as shown in the top half of the figure, boxes clearly denote the stimulus sets and arrows make the hierarchical structure apparent. Level 0

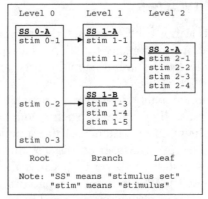

Graphical Format Showing Tree Structure

```
      Level 0        Level 1        Level 2

      SS 0-A         SS 1-A
      stim 0-1       stim 1-1
                                    SS 2-A
                     stim 1-2       stim 2-1
                                    stim 2-2
                                    stim 2-3
                                    stim 2-4

                     SS 1-B
      stim 0-2       stim 1-3
                     stim 1-4
                     stim 1-5

      stim 0-3
```

Standard Textual Format

Figure 7.2   Generic functionality tree.

is clearly the root of the tree, all intermediate levels are branches, and the locally deepest levels in each branch are leaves. Leaf stimulus sets are distinct from branches only in that the stimuli in a leaf stimulus set do not activate any other stimuli; that is, they have no NSR response.

When drawn textually, as shown in the bottom half of the figure, the graphical boxes and arrows are eliminated but the functionality tree is otherwise identical. Horizontal (row) and vertical (column) alignments must be rigorously maintained as these tabular alignments now convey the stimulus set groupings and hierarchical structure without the help (or crutch) of any graphics. With a little practice, the textual format is just as readable as the graphical form, but is much faster and easier to create and maintain. Unlike the graphical format, which requires a graphical drawing tool, a textual functionality tree can be created with a spreadsheet or even a simple text editor. More important, the time saved by not drawing boxes and arrows is substantial, particularly when modifying and updating a functionality tree, which is the mode maintainers of the program will be in for as much as 80 percent of the life of the software. For these

Listing 7.1   Stimulus Sets of Generic Functionality Tree

SS 0-A	SS 1-A	SS 1-B	SS 2-A
stim 0-1	stim 1-1	stim 1-3	stim 2-1
stim 0-2	stim 1-2	stim 1-4	stim 2-2
stim 0-3		stim 1-5	stim 2-3
			stim 2-4

reasons, Freedom recommends that textual notation be used as the standard format for a functionality tree, at least until such time as specialized tools for rapidly drawing and modifying graphical functionality trees become available.

Exactly what information does a functionality tree convey?

Four stimulus sets—generically named SS 0 – A, SS 1 – A, SS 1 – B, and SS 2 – A—are defined by the functionality tree in Figure 7.2. (In an actual project, the stimulus sets and stimuli would have names that are semantically meaningful to the application. Generic "number names" are used here for illustrative purposes only.) The functionality tree indicates the four stimulus sets consist of the stimuli listed in Listing 7.1.

The NSR activation relationship is captured in the relative arrangement of the stimulus sets. If a stimulus in a Level n SS activates a Level $n + 1$ SS, the Level $n + 1$ SS is drawn such that its first stimulus is horizontally level with the triggering Level n stimulus. For example, SS 1 – A is triggered by stim 0 – 1 in SS 0 – A. Therefore, stim 1 – 1, the first stimulus in SS 1 – A, is horizontally aligned to be level with the triggering stim 0 – 1.

Other stimuli in the triggering Level n SS are moved downward so they are horizontally below the triggered Level $n + 1$ SS, thus avoiding the appearance that the nontriggering stimuli might be involved with triggering the stimulus set. In Figure 7.2, for example, stim 0 – 2 and 0 – 3 are moved vertically downward below the horizontal row of SS 1 – A, thereby avoiding any appearance that they may be involved in triggering SS 1 – A. As can be seen in the example, moving them downward also brings them into open rows, which are then available for aligning other SS triggered by these stimuli. For example, stim 0 – 2 activates SS 1 – B, which can be horizontally aligned with stim 0 – 2 because that stimulus has been dropped to a row below SS 1 – A. Likewise, stim 0 – 3 is dropped below SS 1 – B into an open row. Because stim 0 – 3 does not activate any stimulus sets, the row occupied by stim 0 – 3 is left open.

Its hierarchical structure imparts the following semantics to this example functionality tree.

1. When the application is first started, only the stimuli shown at Level 0 are active. Hence, SS 0 – A is the only stimulus set active when the program is launched.

2. If stim 0 – 1 is received, part of its externally visible response is to activate SS 1 – A.
3. If stim 0 – 2 is received, part of its externally visible response is to activate SS 1-B.
4. If stim 0 – 3 is received, it does NOT activate any additional stimuli.
5. If stim 1 – 2 is received, part of its externally visible response is to activate SS 2 – A. Note that stim 1 – 2 cannot be received until stim 0 – 1 is received.

Thus, the semantics of a functionality tree defines:

1. All stimulus sets
2. The stimuli that comprise each stimulus set
3. Which stimuli activate which other stimulus sets, that is, partial NSR responses

The semantics of a functionality tree does *not* specify:

1. Stimulus deactivation
2. Stimulus activation in addition to the indicated stimulus set(s)
3. Any response other than stimulus set activation

The complete response behavior is the purview of the behavior table notation. Behavior tables are covered in Chapter 10.

7.6 Example Problem: Programmatic Interface Functionality Tree

While identifying the stimuli for the human user and programmatic interfaces of the Furmasco furniture inventory system, the shipping department development team simultaneously arranges the stimulus sets into a functionality tree. Let's peer over their shoulders and see how they go about it.

The inventory system includes a read-only programmatic interface to the app server. Recall that the development team used the quality requirements to help decide that a command-data stream is the best protocol for this purpose for their application. Listing 7.2 shows the inventory system command-data stimulus sets from the previous chapter. The command-data stream contains command stimuli at two levels, which group into two command stimulus sets. It also contains three data stimulus sets. The team uses a straightforward three-step process to organize these stimulus sets into a functionality tree.

Listing 7.2 Inventory System Send Protocol Stimulus Sets

Cmd Type SS	Categ SS	Type SS	Furn Data SS
01	category	type	12
02			13
03			14
10			15
			19
Descrip SS			
description			

Step 1

Place the stimulus set with the highest-level commands at relative Level 0, which is the level at which these stimuli first become active.

Cmd Type SS contains the highest-level command stimuli, stimuli 01 through 10, of the command-data stream. They place Cmd Type SS at relative Level 0, which is also absolute Level 0 because these stimuli will be active when the program first starts.

Step 2

Place lower-level command stimulus sets, if any, in successively lower columns based on the NSR triggering response of Level $n - 1$ command stimuli. Horizontally align the first stimulus of the SS with its triggering Level $n - 1$ stimulus.

Furniture Data SS contains the lower-level commands, stimuli 12 through 19. This stimulus set will be activated by the "description" stimulus of Descrip SS. Thus, the team places Furniture Data SS one level below its triggering stimulus "description." Stimulus 12, the first stimulus in the SS, is horizontally aligned with the triggering stimulus. Note that Descript SS itself has not yet been placed in the tree.

Step 3

Place data stimulus sets one level below their triggering command stimuli. Horizontally align the first stimulus of the SS with its triggering Level $n - 1$ command stimulus.

The three stimulus sets Categ SS, Type SS, and Descrip SS are placed at Level 2, horizontally aligned with their triggering Level 1 command stimuli.

The resulting functionality tree for the inventory command-data programmatic interface is shown in Listing 7.3.

Listing 7.3   Inventory System Programmatic Functionality Tree

Level 0	Level 1	Level 3
Cmd Type SS	Categ SS	
01	category	
	Type SS	
02	type	
03		
	Descrip SS	Furn Data SS
10	description	12
		13
		14
		15
		19

7.7 Example Problem: Reverse Engineering the External Interface Architecture

In the previous chapter, we saw that the shipping department development team created a functionality screen for the human user interface to the Furmasco furniture inventory system. They did this by consulting with the users of the existing inventory system to be replaced. Let's see what they did in more detail.

Before consulting with the users, the development team decided to reverse engineer the human user requirements architecture of the existing system. With Freedom, reverse engineering the requirements architecture is possible, even if the original requirements, design, and code are not available (fortunately for the team, because the existing system is proprietary). By Freedom's black box definition, requirements are literally there for all to see, so reverse engineering them is really just a matter of systematic observation.[1]

The team starts by observing the screens of the existing inventory system. Its human interface consists of the three graphical screens shown in Figures 7.3 through 7.5. They identify the human user stimulus sets by noting the stimulus groupings on the screens.

The team decides that first screen consists of one stimulus set of two stimuli, add furniture and view furniture. The second screen, for adding furniture, appears to consist of three stimulus sets based on physical grouping: classification selection, furniture data, and return to main. The team decides the third screen, for viewing furniture, consists of four stimulus sets based on physical grouping: view entire inventory, view by category, view by type, and return to main.

With the stimulus sets identified, the functionality tree is formed by observing the New Stimulus Response (NSR) relationships among the

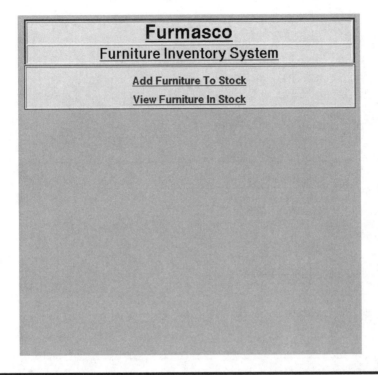

Figure 7.3   Old inventory system Screen 1.

stimuli. It is very simple. When the program starts the first screen is active, so Main SS is at Level 0 of the functionality tree. Its "add furniture" stimulus activates all the stimuli of the second screen, so all three of the Add Furniture screens' stimulus sets are placed at Level 1 aligned next to the Level 0 "add furniture" stimulus. Similarly, the "view furniture" stimulus triggers activation of all stimuli of the four stimulus sets of the View Furniture screen, so these are placed at Level 1 aligned with the "view furniture" stimulus. The resulting functionality tree for the existing furniture inventory system is depicted in Listing 7.4.

7.8 Example Problem Functionality Tree

With the reverse-engineered functionality tree and actual screens of the existing inventory system in hand, the team consults with the users regarding a functionality screen for the new inventory system. They start by asking the users a standard requirements kickoff question:

> What do you want the first screen to look like when the program starts up?

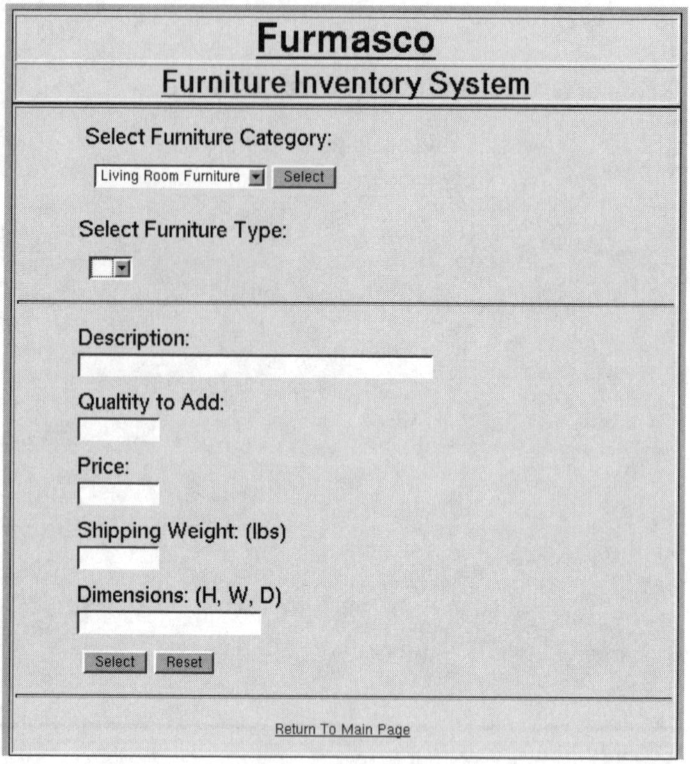

Figure 7.4 Old inventory system Screen 2.

The users, acclimated to the current system, draw sketches of the existing system with desired improvements, such as a "modify" option. Further discussion of needs, desires, and alternatives for achieving them finally results in the functionality screen shown in the previous chapter as Listing 6.7.

The new functionality screen consists of a single window, rather than three screens or windows like the existing inventory system. Per Freedom guidelines, the decision to use a single window is reached by using the quality requirements to analyze the multiple-window versus single-window alternatives. The results of this trade-off analysis are shown in Table 7.1. The single-window alternative wins in every respect. However, as some on the team are quick to point out, this is only because the human stimuli are few in number. For larger numbers of stimuli, both human factors and maintainability considerations would favor multiple windows.

When designing the protocol, or look and feel, of the new layout, the team is careful to physically delineate the stimulus sets, of which there

Figure 7.5   Old inventory system Screen 3.

are four: Furniture Classification; List of Furniture; Furniture Data; and the three buttons view, add, and modify. (The message area at the bottom of the window, being display-only, contains no stimulus sources and so is not a stimulus set.) Some team members state that the new layout also moves all stimulus sets to Level 0 of the functionality tree because they are now all visible at once. However, the team lead points out that this is not the case.

> Team Lead: From the user's perspective, a software system is a collection of interrelated external interface components called stimulus sets. A functionality tree is an easy way to define the stimulus sets and their hierarchical relationship. It aids developers in getting a grasp on the system by showing how root, branch, and leaf stimulus sets connect to form the complete external interface. Can anyone tell me what is the first step in creating a functionality tree?
>
> Team Member: Identify the stimuli and stimulus sets.

Listing 7.4   Old Inventory System Functionality Tree

```
Level 0          Level 1
Main SS          View All SS
view furniture   view entire

                 View by Categ SS
                 list of categ
                 select

                 View by Type SS
                 list of types
                 select

                 Main Return SS
                 return to main

                 Classification SS
add furniture    list of categ
                 list of types
                 select

                 Furniture Data SS
                 description
                 quantity to add
                 price
                 shipping wt
                 dimensions
                 select
                 reset

                 Main Return SS
                 return to main
```

Team Lead: Close, but not quite. Also, we already have the stimulus sets. So what is the first step in creating the functionality tree?

Another Team Member: Identify the Level 0, or root, stimuli: those active when the program starts up.

Team Lead: Right! What stimulus sets in our functionality screen are active—not just visible, but *active*—when the program starts up?

Discussion ensues regarding the triggering relationships among the various stimuli and stimulus sets. The List of Furniture SS becomes active when a furniture classification category is selected, so the List of Furniture SS is not Level 0. Furniture Data SS displays data in response to selection of an item in the List of Furniture SS, so Furniture Data is not Level 0

Table 7.1 Inventory System Functionality Screen Trade-Off

Rank	Quality Attribute	Multiple Windows	Single Window
1	Functionality	Identical (same stimuli)	Identical (same stimuli)
2	Reliability	Unaffected	Unaffected
3	Maintainability	Good: SS in windows allow reqmts. encapsulation	Better: fewer SS to encapsulate = less code
4	Usability	Fair: must navigate layers	Good: no layer navigation
5	Administerability	Unaffected	Unaffected
6	Execution speed	Unaffected	Unaffected
7	Storage demand	Acceptable	Better: due to less code

either. The triggering chain starts with Furniture Classification, so it must be at Level 0. The "quit" stimulus is active on start-up, so it must be at Level 0 also.

What about the view, add, and modify buttons? What do they do?

Team member: They are radio buttons; only one can be selected at once. They control the operation of Furniture Data SS. When "view" is selected, the Furniture Data stimuli are display-only and cannot be used to update the database. When "add" is selected, the Furniture Data stimuli are interpreted as a new furniture record to add to the database. When "modify" is selected, the Furniture Data stimuli are interpreted as an existing furniture record to modify in the database. They are mode control stimuli for Furniture Data. When the program starts up, it is safest to be in "view" mode.

The rest of the team agrees. Because the buttons control mode, they call the three buttons the Mode stimulus set, or Mode SS. Because the buttons are active on program start-up, with the view button selected initially, Mode SS is at Level 0.

Further discussion refines the triggering relationships, and results in the functionality tree shown in Listing 7.5. When drawing this tree, the

Listing 7.5   Inventory System Human User Functionality Tree

```
Level 0              Level 1
Inventory SS
quit

Classification SS    Furniture List SS
list of types        list of furniture
list of categ

Mode SS              Furniture Data SS
add                  description
                     quantity
                     price
                     shipping wt
                     dimensions
                     select
                     reset

                     Furniture Data SS
modify               [description]
                     quantity
                     price
                     [shipping wt]
                     [dimensions]
                     select
                     reset
view

Notes:
1. to delete, modify with negative quantity
```

team takes the liberty of using a gray color to depict deactivation of some Furniture Data SS stimuli in response to the "modify" button. Functionality trees normally do not show stimulus deactivation, but only activation. The team considers grayed stimuli to be an expedient way of remembering the full NSR response to "modify" until the behavior tables are created. The team also includes a note at the bottom of the functionality tree reminding them that a negative "quantity" stimulus will serve to delete furniture from the database, thus avoiding another explicit mode and corresponding button.

This completes the requirements architecture for the inventory system. The external interface architecture appears as two functionality trees. Listing 7.3 shows the functionality tree for the command-data protocol for use by the app server. Listing 7.5 shows the functionality tree for the human user interface. The team decides to leave the functionality tree split into two parts for ease of printing on paper, and for ease of maintenance.

7.9 Alternate Kickoff Approaches

In the example, the development team kicked off their dialogue with the users with the question:

> What do you want the first screen to look like when the program starts up?

However, pure embedded applications have only programmatic interfaces to other systems or the environment, and no human user interface. This question does not apply to them. Moreover, there are no human users to consult. What then?

There is a variation of the kickoff question that can be used in cases where most stimuli originate with external systems or the environment. This question is asked of the customer or the appointed customer point of contact (POC):

> What is the first thing the program should listen for when it first starts up?

This is really the same question as the human user kickoff question, just posed in slightly different terms better suited to programmatic stimuli. The goal is still the same, that is, to identify the Level 0 stimuli, which are the stimuli active on program start-up.

If the POC happens to be another developer who understands functionality trees and Freedom's stimulus–response technique, the question could be phrased more generically as:

> What are the first stimuli and stimulus sets active on program start-up?

These are really three variants of the same question for use in different circumstances. Other variations may also be possible. Regardless of exactly how the kickoff question is phrased, the goal is to engage the customer, user, or POC in a dialogue to discover the stimuli relevant to the application, starting with those that are active first.

In many cases, the customer may quickly conclude we are trying to design the external interface (user or programmatic), when we are actually trying to identify and organize stimuli. This is okay. There is no harm in letting the customer persist in that belief, because it is part of the truth. It is also okay to tell the customer that defining the external interface is equivalent to defining the requirements. Most customers will have no problem with that concept. If the result is a big interface design session, go for it!

7.10 Functionality Tree Neutrality

If we were given the inventory functionality tree in Listing 7.5 without ever having seen it before or knowing how it was obtained, would we be able to answer questions such as the following?

1. Which stimuli are text fields?
2. Which stimuli are buttons?
3. Which stimuli are hardware toggle switches?

The answer is, we should not be able to answer such questions using the functionality tree. When creating a functionality tree, especially when creating it from protocol descriptions such as functionality screens, implementation-specific information should be eliminated to the extent possible. For example, in Listing 7.5, the "view" stimulus could have been written instead as "view button." It was not written as "view button" because to do so would have made the functionality tree more implementation-specific.

In general, functionality trees should avoid names that imply an implementation mechanism such as button, text field, pop-up, and so on. Listings 7.3 and 7.5 use the term "list" in stimulus names, but only in a generic sense to mean a "variable list of stimuli," and not to imply a GUI list component or any other specific implementation mechanism. A counterexample is Listing 6.6, which includes XML-specific angle brackets in the stimulus names. The brackets are necessary to distinguish stimuli, such as <city> and </city>, which would otherwise be indistinguishable.

By keeping functionality trees as implementation neutral as possible, they are better able to fulfill their role as a schematic of the external interface that identifies stimuli and their organization without regard to specific implementation. An implementation neutral functionality tree helps focus mental energy on the required functionality without diverting excessive thought to implementation issues.[2] The urge to place implementation-specific information in the functionality tree can be reduced by developing notations such as functionality screens and behavior tables in parallel with the functionality tree. Any thoughts about implementation can then be recorded immediately in the proper notation. For example, the inventory development team can avoid the crutch of graying some stimuli in the functionality tree of Listing 7.5 by developing behavior tables in parallel with the functionality tree.

References

1. Reverse engineering is constrained to what can actually be observed. For example, the human user interface can be observed directly, but the interface to an external system may require instrumenting the external system to capture traffic to the system.
2. Of course, some thought must be given to the implementability. Requirements should not be excessively expensive, or even impossible, to implement!

Chapter 8

Reusable Requirements

8.1 Chapter Overview

The previous chapter describes a functionality tree variously as (1) an entity-relationship model that organizes stimulus sets into a horizontal hierarchy based on the New Stimulus Response relationship, (2) the external interface architecture of the system, and (3) an implementation-independent schematic of the external interface. As if all this were not enough, a functionality tree is also (4) the mechanism for identifying opportunities for requirements reuse. This chapter discusses how opportunities for requirements reuse can be identified in the context of a functionality tree, as well as the general nature of reusable requirements components.

The role of requirements reuse in the Freedom requirements process is illustrated by the shaded box in Figure 8.1. Reusable requirements components are stored in a logical reuse library and reused in new software, similar to the way reusable design components are currently stored and reused in the form of Application Program Interface (API) packages. However, the way in which reusable requirements components are identified is more systematic than the manner in which current reusable design APIs are conceived.

8.2 Repetitive and Reusable Stimulus Sets

When creating a functionality tree, a stimulus set (SS) will sometimes be activated by more than one stimulus. In order to preserve the tree structure

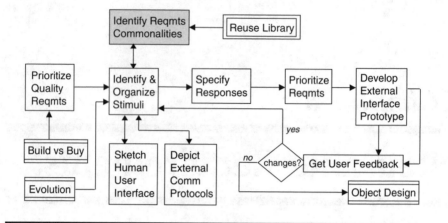

Figure 8.1 **Reusable requirements in the requirements process.**

Listing 8.1 **Generic Functionality Tree with Explicit Repetition**

```
Level 0        Level 1        Level 2


SS 0-A         SS 1-A
stim 0-1       stim 1-1

                              SS 2-A
               stim 1-2       stim 2-1
                              stim 2-2
                              stim 2-3
                              stim 2-4
               SS 2-A
stim 0-2       stim 2-1
               stim 2-2
               stim 2-3
               stim 2-4

stim 0-3

Note:  "SS" means "stimulus set"
       "stim" means "stimulus"
```

of the functionality tree, such multiply activated SSs should be repeated, appearing to the right of each triggering stimulus. The first occurrence of a repetitive SS must be specified in its entirety as usual, but subsequent occurrences repeat only the stimulus set name and use a phrase such as "reused SS" in place of the list of stimuli.

For example, in the generic functionality tree of Listing 8.1, stimulus set SS 2 – A appears twice due to being activated by both stim 1 – 2 and stim 0 – 2. This makes SS 2 – A a repetitive stimulus set; that is, it is

Listing 8.2   Generic Functionality Tree with Repetitive SS

Level 0	Level 1	Level 2
SS 0-A	**SS 1-A**	
stim 0-1	stim 1-1	
		SS 2-A
	stim 1-2	stim 2-1
		stim 2-2
		stim 2-3
		stim 2-4
	SS 2-A	
stim 0-2	(reused SS)	
stim 0-3		

repeated in the functionality tree. As a result, the functionality tree of Listing 8.1 is modified to the form shown in Listing 8.2. In this (more correct) functionality tree, SS 2 – A occurs in its entirety only in its first occurrence. In subsequent occurrences, such as after the stim 0 – 2, the SS name is repeated for identification but its constituent stimuli are replaced by "reused SS" indicating that this stimulus set has been defined previously. There are several advantages to recording subsequent occurrences by reference in this manner.

1. Should the list of stimuli ever change, only the first occurrence of the repetitive stimulus set needs to be changed, all other occurrences will implicitly be changed via reference to the first (a simple case of inheritance). This makes maintenance of the functionality tree easier.
2. Potential recording problems associated with recursion are avoided.
3. The referential placeholder serves as an indication that the referenced stimulus set has greater than single-use utility; that is, the stimulus set may be a candidate for requirements reuse.

A repetitive stimulus set such as SS 2 – A might also be reusable. The distinction is as follows.

> A repetitive stimulus set is activated by two or more different stimuli of an application.
> A reusable stimulus set is activated by stimuli in two or more different applications.

Not all repetitive stimulus sets are reusable; that is, just because a stimulus set is activated from multiple places in a single application does not necessarily imply it will have utility in an entirely different application.

For example, SS 2 – A is clearly repetitive due to being activated by two different stimuli. However, is it reusable? That is, is SS 2 – A useful in an entirely different application? It depends on its utility.

For SS 2 – A to be reusable, its constituent stimuli, stim 2 – 1 through stim 2 – 4, must be useful in other applications besides the current system. Moreover, the response behavior for these stimuli must also be the same across multiple applications. This hints at another feature of repetitive and reusable stimulus sets.

In addition to being a cue for potential reusability, repetitive and reusable stimulus sets reduce the number of behavior tables that need to be specified. The response behavior of the stimuli must be the same for all occurrences in the functionality tree or, at least, be configurable within specified limits. Thus, only one behavior table needs to be specified for a repetitive or reusable stimulus set, regardless of the number of repetitions in the functionality tree.

Just as not all repetitive SS are reusable, not all reusable SS need be repetitive. The developers may anticipate that a SS will be useful in other programs, even if it only appears once in the functionality tree. An example might be a log-in window. The stimuli of a reusable SS should be chosen to provide generically robust functionality, even if not all the resulting stimuli are needed by the current application.

Both forms are advantageous economically. Reusable SS are economically rewarding across multiple projects, and repetitive SS are cost-effective for the single project. The key characteristic of both is that they are always recognizable by stimulus set repetition, whether it be within a single functionality tree or among the functionality trees of different applications.

8.3 Reusable Requirements Components

At the level of detail of the functionality tree, a reusable SS appears only as a stimulus set name and an associated list of stimuli. How might a reusable SS be manifested further along in the development process?

After development of the functionality tree, responses are defined for each stimulus. As mentioned above, only one behavior specification needs to be developed for a reusable SS inasmuch as the behavior is also reusable, perhaps with configuration within well-specified limits. Because the behavior specification does not change, design and implementation also need be performed only once for a reusable SS. Thus, a reusable SS grows into a complete reusable requirements component consisting of requirements specification, design specification, implementing code, test code, and associated documentation.

Storage of a reusable requirements component in a reuse library is a matter of storing its constituent parts as a coherent set. Of the various parts, code and documentation are routinely stored in reuse libraries today. Requirements and design specifications are usually not, but there are no technical barriers to doing so. Physically, a reuse library may be anything from a specific set of directories in the file system to a specialized configuration management tool. Any of these alternatives can store textual and binary files, so any can store code, documentation, and specifications such as the functionality tree and behavior tables. Storing the components of a reusable requirements component as a coherent set could be as simple as zipping the components into a single compressed archive file, or as complex as creating a special configuration management tool that maintains its own links among the components.

Regardless of how it is stored, pulling a reusable requirements specification from a reuse library is much like pulling a jellyfish from the water. Normally, only the above-water head of the jellyfish is visible. This head is analogous to the requirements notations of the reusable requirements component: the functionality tree, behavior tables, and external protocol specifications. However, grasping the externally visible head (requirements notations) and "lifting" reveals a long train of attached tentacles, which correspond to the design and implementation notations including design specifications, implementation code, regression test code, and code-level documentation for the reusable requirements component.

As a result, reusable requirements components are extremely high leverage. If an application could be built entirely from reusable requirements components the effort of design, coding, regression testing, and code-level documentation would all be eliminated. The only necessary tasks would be creation of the functionality tree (requirements architecture) by splicing together the smaller functionality subtrees of each component, writing and performing requirements-level validation tests, and writing the user manual. As estimated in Appendix B, development cost would be reduced by over two-thirds and total software life-cycle cost would be cut by 30 percent. Moreover, as explained in the appendix, these estimates are conservative. Like exploration of a new world, no one really knows what the benefits of requirements reuse will really be until we actually go there. However, if history is any guide, the actual benefits will likely be different from, and greater than, what we might expect.

8.4 Example Reusable Requirements Component

Figure 8.2 is a screen shot of an instance of FileDialog. FileDialog is a stock Java abstract window toolkit (awt) component for traversing a

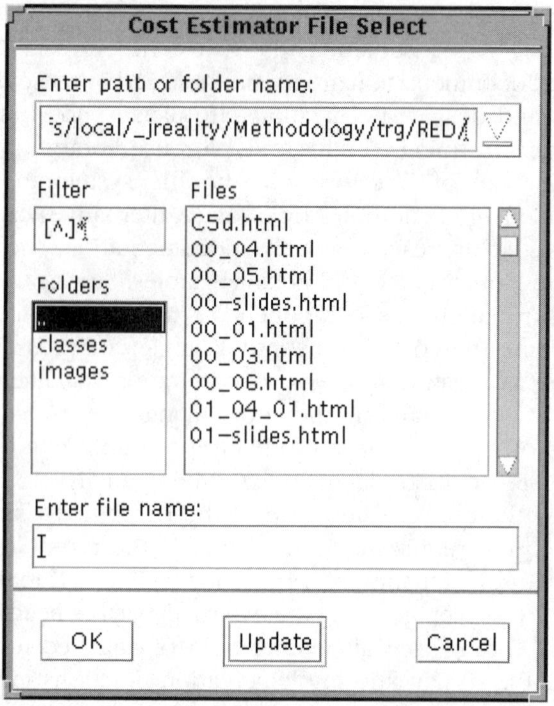

Cost Estimator File Select

Enter path or folder name:

`s/local/_jreality/Methodology/trg/RED/`

Filter

`[^.]*`

Files

C5d.html
00_04.html
00_05.html
00-slides.html
00_01.html
00_03.html
00_06.html
01_04_01.html
01-slides.html

Folders

`..`
classes
images

Enter file name:

| OK | Update | Cancel |

Figure 8.2   FileDialog Human Interface protocol.

Listing 8.3   FileDialog Functionality Tree

Level 0	Level 1	Level 2	Level 3
FileDialog	**Folders**	**Files**	**FileName**
path list	direc list	file list	filename
filter			
Buttons			
ok			
update			
cancel			

directory tree and selecting a file. FileDialog has been around for years. Most people consider it one of the more unassuming of the many reusable Java API components.

From the perspective of Freedom, FileDialog consists of five interacting stimulus sets, as shown in the functionality tree of Listing 8.3. When a FileDialog first appears, all five stimulus sets are usually active. Therefore, it might seem that all five SS should appear at Level 0 of the FileDialog functionality tree. However, in the "worst" (or least-initialized) case, a FileDialog might launch with only the three buttons, path list, and filter fields active and no stimuli displayed in the other stimulus sets. Thus, the SS activation chain shown in Listing 8.3 is a more general representation of the FileDialog external interface architecture based on the NSR stimulus activation relationship. If used in a functionality tree, all instances of FileDialog, including the first instance, would use the "reused SS" referential notation. This is because FileDialog is defined and maintained outside the context of any application. Thus, all occurrences in an application functionality tree are referential to the external definition.

FileDialog is widely recognized as a reusable component because its utility spans multiple applications. What is not widely recognized is that FileDialog is a reusable *requirements* component because it is a stimulus set (actually a collection of stimulus sets) that encapsulates a complete software external interface including stimulus, response, and protocol.[1] Of course, being a Java component, FileDialog contains all implementing code and code-level documentation. If one were to imagine FileDialog as a reusable requirements jellyfish, it might look something like Figure 8.3. This figure is based on an analysis of the actual classes that compose FileDialog, but is incomplete due to space limitations of the figure; that is, the actual length of the "tentacles" is greater than shown. Clearly, using FileDialog results in substantial design and implementation leverage, yet FileDialog is not considered a very exciting component! Imagine the leverage of something more interesting, perhaps a reusable requirements component from an inventory application.

8.5 Example Problem Reusable Requirements

While developing the functionality tree of Listing 7.5, the Furmasco inventory system development team notices that Furniture Data SS appears twice due to being activated by both the "add" and "modify" stimuli. They quickly realize that subsequent occurrences of repetitive stimulus sets should be by reference. Consequently, they modify the functionality tree of Listing 7.5 to appear as shown in Listing 8.4. In this corrected version, Furniture Data SS occurs in its entirety only at its first occurrence. In the subsequent occurrence, adjacent to the "modify" stimulus, the name of the stimulus set is repeated but its constituent stimuli are replaced by the notation "(reused SS)" indicating that this is a repetitive instance of a previously defined stimulus set.

Furniture Data SS is clearly repetitive, but the team must also decide if it is also reusable.

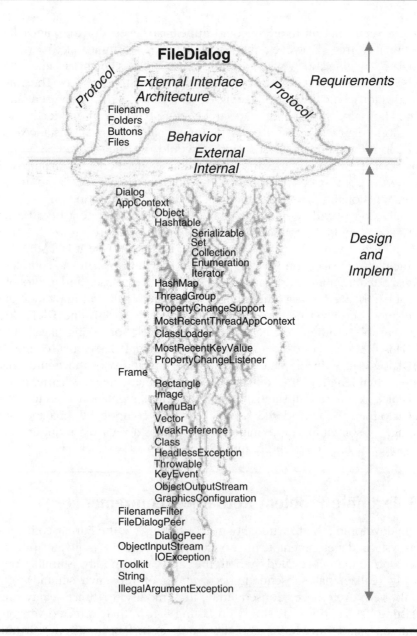

Figure 8.3   FileDialog reusable requirements jellyfish.

That is, is Furniture Data SS useful in applications other than the Furmasco furniture inventory system?

Possibly. The constituent stimuli—description, quantity, price, shipping weight, dimensions, reset, and select—appear to be applicable to any inventory system, not just furniture. Although the response behavior for

Listing 8.4   Inventory System Functionality Tree with Reuse

Level 0	Level 1
Inventory SS	
quit	
Classification SS	**Furniture List SS**
list of types	list of furniture
list of categ	
Mode SS	**Furniture Data SS**
add	description
	quantity
	price
	shipping wt
	dimensions
	select
	reset
	Furniture Data SS
modify	(reused SS)
view	

Notes:
1. to delete, modify with negative quantity

these stimuli has yet to be specified in detail, the team knows the response in general will be to store the values in a database, as implied by the triggering stimuli "add" and "modify." Storing values in a database is also applicable across different applications. Thus, it appears to the team that Furniture Data SS is not just repetitive, but is a reusable stimulus set with utility in applications other than their own inventory program. The referential notation "(reused SS)" is therefore accurate and need not be changed to, say, "(repetitive SS)." When the time comes to design and implement Furniture Data SS, the team will not be adverse to maximizing its utility beyond the needs of their own application.

References

1. Most other awt components are reusable *design* components because they implement stimuli, not stimulus sets, and their response behavior is deliberately left unspecified; that is, they do not implement a complete software external interface.

Chapter 9

Incremental Development

9.1 Chapter Overview

Freedom's box-based concept model offers much technical guidance but little project management guidance. Thus, Freedom is primarily a technical methodology rather than a management methodology. Far from being a weakness, management neutrality permits Freedom to be used with most management processes and life-cycle models such as spiral, incremental, evolutionary, waterfall, and others.

Although Freedom strives to be management neutral, complete separation of technical and management concerns is not feasible. This chapter describes Freedom's approach to requirements prioritization, a step in the requirements process necessary for support of incremental, evolutionary, and similar life-cycle models.

The position of requirements prioritization in the Freedom requirements process is illustrated by the shaded box in Figure 9.1. In practice, requirements should be prioritized after the responses to all stimuli are specified because full knowledge of the required behavior is available to help guide prioritization decisions. Freedom records requirements priorities in the context of the functionality tree, therefore the topic is being covered now as the last of several chapters describing functionality trees.

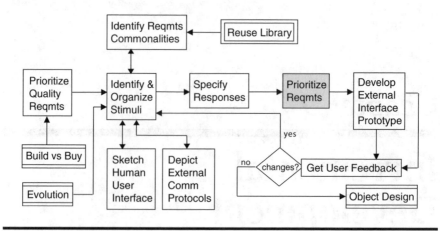

Figure 9.1 Requirements prioritization in the requirements process

9.2 Requirements Prioritization

After the functionality tree is created, the size and scope of the project become more apparent. In general, the larger the functionality tree, the larger the project and the longer the time to completion. If the customer requires early availability of crucial capabilities, the functionality tree may be used as a basis for prioritization of the requirements and associated planning and scheduling of multiple releases. If desired by the customer, the requirements (stimulus sets and associated behavior tables) may be prioritized into release groups based on their importance or immediacy of need. Design and implementation are then performed repetitively for each release group, starting with the highest priority. Requirements prioritization allows Freedom to be easily adapted to incremental, evolutionary, frequent release, and similar management methodologies.

A functionality tree can be used to prioritize requirements in two steps.

Step 1. Prioritize Lowest-Level Stimuli

Lowest-level stimuli are the "leaf" stimuli of the functionality tree; they are stimuli that do *not* activate a stimulus set. Most of the actual functionality of the application resides in the response behavior of lower-level stimuli. Therefore, requirements are prioritized starting at the lowest levels of the functionality tree. Each lowest-level stimulus–response pair is examined and assigned a priority classification or, equivalently, a release number based on the time-criticality to the customer of the capability inherent in the requirement (stimulus–response pair).

For example, in the sample functionality tree in Listing 9.1, the lowest-level stimuli are stim 0 – 3, stim 1 – 1, and stim 2 – 1 through stim 2 – 4

Listing 9.1 Generic Functionality Tree with Requirements Prioritization

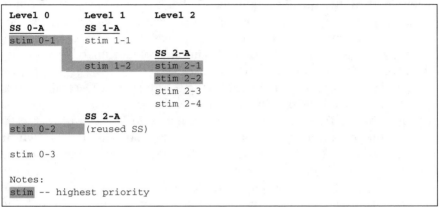

```
Level 0        Level 1        Level 2
SS 0-A         SS 1-A
stim 0-1       stim 1-1
                              SS 2-A
               stim 1-2       stim 2-1
                              stim 2-2
                              stim 2-3
                              stim 2-4
               SS 2-A
stim 0-2       (reused SS)

stim 0-3

Notes:
stim -- highest priority
```

because these do not activate any stimulus sets. Furthermore, assume the customer needs the functionality of stim 2 – 1 and stim 2 – 2 as soon as possible. These two stimuli would then be flagged as highest priority, indicated by being highlighted.

Step 2. Prioritize Upper-Level Stimuli

Upper-level stimuli are the "branch" stimuli of the functionality tree; they are stimuli that activate another stimulus set. Because upper-level stimuli lie on the activation path to lower-level stimuli, the priority of upper-level stimuli depends on the priority of the lower-level stimuli they activate. Specifically, the priority of an upper-level stimulus is the same as the highest-priority stimulus of all the stimuli that it directly activates.

The result is a hierarchy of "threads of priority" running through the functionality tree. Where threads of different priority value merge, the higher value continues up to higher levels of the tree. Inevitably, at least one stimulus at Level 0 will be of the highest priority, so at least some of the Level 0 stimulus set(s) will always be included in the initial release, or first release group.

This prioritization approach can result in different priorities being assigned to different stimuli in the same stimulus set; that is, different stimuli in a given SS may be assigned to different release groups. How should stimuli scheduled for a future release be handled in the current release? There are at least two approaches:

1. Do not implement deferred stimuli. The release contains implemented stimuli only.
2. Implement deferred stimuli in a way that makes it clear to the user that the stimuli are not active (e.g., "grayed out").

As with any other development decision, which approach to use is determined by the quality requirements. For the default quality requirements, usability would favor Option 2 because a visual placeholder for deferred stimuli helps notify users that these capabilities are not forgotten, just not yet implemented. Option 2 also improves maintainability, reducing work for the developers of future releases.

Continuing with the example of Listing 9.1, the upper-level stimuli that activate the two high-priority lowest-level stimuli are also flagged as highest priority. This includes stim 1 – 2 and stim 0 – 2, which directly activate the high-priority lowest-level stimuli, and stim 0 – 1, which activates stim 1 – 2 and is therefore on the highest-priority path. Like the lowest-level stimuli, these upper-level stimuli are flagged as highest priority by being highlighted. The requirements to be included in the initial release are now clearly indicated by the highlighted threads running through the functionality tree.

9.3 Example Problem Requirements Priorities

After developing the functionality tree and associated behavior tables (see Chapter 10), the Furmasco inventory system development team prioritizes the inventory system requirements. The shipping department personnel on the team state their first use of the new inventory system will be to transfer all the inventory data from the old proprietary system to the new inventory system. A shipping department study concludes that the quickest way to effect the transfer is to manually re-enter the current inventory data into the new system using the human user interface. Thus, the "add" functionality needs to be operational as soon as possible to expedite transfer of the data.

The team refers to Figure 8.4, the functionality tree for the system. All stimuli of Furniture Data SS must be in the initial release, along with the triggering "add" stimulus of Mode SS. The team highlights these stimuli to denote they are highest priority. Also, although not apparent from the functionality tree, the behavior tables indicate that classification data for each inventory item must be stored in the database along with the data in the entry fields of Furniture Data SS. This results in the two Classification SS stimuli being highlighted as high priority. Also, a way is needed to verify the data are entered and saved correctly in the database. The team agrees the easiest way to do this is to implement the Furniture List SS stimuli. Therefore, the Furniture List SS stimuli are added to the highlighted high-priority threads. The resulting priority-annotated functionality tree appears in Listing 9.2.

Listing 9.2 Inventory System Requirements Priorities

```
Level 0            Level 1
Inventory SS
quit

Classification SS  Furniture List SS
list of types      list of furniture

list of categ

Mode SS            Furniture Data SS
add                description
                   quantity
                   price
                   shipping wt
                   dimensions
                   select
                   reset

                   Furniture Data SS
modify             (reused SS)
view

Notes:
1. to delete, modify with negative quantity
2. stimulus -- highest priority
```

Chapter 10

Responses and Behavior Tables

10.1 Chapter Overview

This chapter examines the recording of required response behavior. First, the different types of responses are identified. Next, a tabular format called a "behavior table" is introduced. Behavior tables serve as containers for recording required responses in a regular and systematic way. Finally, several types of languages for response recording are examined and compared, and the language recommended for use with Freedom is identified and explained.

Behavior specification must follow stimulus identification because required behavior is always a response to a stimulus. This relationship of responses to stimuli is evident in Figure 10.1 by the location of the shaded box in the Freedom requirements process.

10.2 Types of Responses

A response is defined as a reaction or possible reaction to a stimulus. A response may be complex, such as generating a three-dimensional scene. Or, it may be simple such as echoing a datum as it is typed, or storing the datum in memory. The null response (do nothing) is also a possible response to a stimulus.

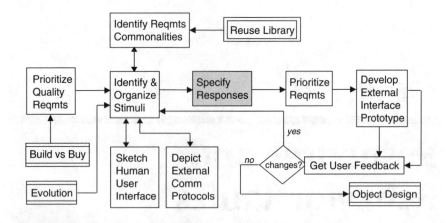

Figure 10.1 Response specification in the requirements process.

Although the complexity of a response is significant, responses may be more fruitfully characterized by their visibility, desirability, and prescriptiveness.

10.2.1 Response Visibility

There are two kinds of responses based on their visibility to the external world: external and internal.

External responses are detectable outside the software system black box, as illustrated in Figure 10.2. External responses are sent to the same places where stimuli originate, that is, human users, external systems, or the environment. However, the destination for a response need not always match the source of its triggering stimulus. For example, a human user stimulus can cause a response to be sent to an external system. Along with their triggering stimuli and implementing external protocols, external responses constitute requirements information.

Internal responses are those that are detectable only within the system black box. Such responses are generated by the modules that comprise the black box, as illustrated in Figure 10.2, and are sent to other modules.[1] Internal responses constitute design and implementation information. Internal responses that appear in a requirements specification are treated either as statements of nonbinding guidance if specified by developers, or as design and implementation (D&I) constraints if specified by the customer (see Section 3.5).

The total response to a stimulus is the union of its external and internal responses.

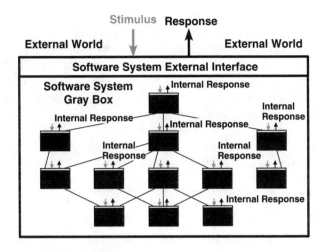

Figure 10.2 Internal responses.

10.2.2 Response Desirability

There are two kinds of responses based on desirability: normal and error responses.

A normal response is the expected response to a stimulus in normal operation. A normal response is required; that is, all stimuli have a normal response. This includes stimuli of test suites that test error behavior, for which the normal response will be the (correct) triggering of an error response. A normal response may be external (requirements) or internal (D&I).

A new stimulus response (NSR) is a kind of normal response that activates or deactivates one or more stimuli. It is permissible for a stimulus to have only a NSR because a NSR is a type of normal response, or to have no NSR because a NSR is optional. A NSR is treated as a special category of normal response due to being the relationship inherent in the functionality tree and external interface architecture (see Section 7.3). If the functionality tree shows that a stimulus activates a stimulus set, that stimulus must have a matching NSR in the behavior table; that is, the recorded response behavior must agree with the functionality tree. Because it is externally detectable, a NSR is always requirements information; there is no such thing as an internal NSR.

An error response is a response that indicates a deviation from normal operation, for example, triggering a stimulus at an inappropriate time or, for data stimuli, with inappropriate data values. A stimulus need not have an error response; an error response is optional. It is also conditional:

when present, an error response must occur in the context of decision logic. An error response may be external (requirements) or internal (D&I).

An error NSR response is a logical possibility (such as activation of an error message stimulus set) but is not significant enough to warrant a separate category. Thus, there are three types of responses based on desirability: normal, NSR, and error. The total response to a stimulus is the union of its normal, NSR, and error responses.

10.2.3 Response Prescriptiveness

There are two kinds of responses based on prescriptiveness: binding and guidance responses.

Binding responses are specified by the customer. Binding responses must be implemented by the developers exactly as specified unless a change to the response is explicitly agreed to by the customer. External responses (requirements) are always binding responses. Internal responses (D&I) may or may not be binding depending on who specifies them.

Guidance responses are specified at the discretion of the development team. They may be changed at will by the development team using whatever specification control mechanisms the team desires or, perhaps, are imposed on the team by a project management methodology external to Freedom. Guidance responses are completely nonbinding on the development team and need not be implemented as specified, or even implemented at all.

The only important responses to Freedom are the binding responses. Only the binding responses need be met. Any nonbinding responses may be implemented in support of the binding responses at the discretion of the development team. Thus, the total response to a stimulus consists of its binding responses and, optionally, some or all of its guidance responses.

10.2.4 Response Classification

The above response attributes may be combined to produce what has been variously called a "classification list"[2] or an "option profile."[3] The first step in combining the attributes is to list the attributes in sequence similar to digit placeholders in a number, as shown in Listing 10.1. The second step is to enumerate all possible combinations of the attributes while noting which combinations are invalid, and why. The result of this step is shown in Listing 10.2. The last step is to delete all invalid combinations to produce the final response classification list shown in Listing 10.3.

The response categories shown in the response classification list are instrumental in the construction of behavior tables.

Listing 10.1 Response Attributes

Visibility	Desirability	Prescriptive
external	normal	binding
internal	NSR	guidance
	error	

Listing 10.2 Response Attribute Combinations

Visibility	Desirability	Prescriptive	Response Category
external	normal	binding	Normal
external	normal	guidance	invalid (Note 1)
external	NSR	binding	NSR
external	NSR	guidance	invalid (Note 1)
external	error	binding	Error
external	error	guidance	invalid (Note 1)
internal	normal	binding	D&I Constraint, normal
internal	normal	guidance	D&I Guidance, normal
internal	NSR	binding	invalid (Note 2)
internal	NSR	guidance	invalid (Note 2)
internal	error	binding	D&I Constraint, error
internal	error	guidance	D&I Guidance, error

Notes:
1. external (requirement) is always binding
2. NSR is always external

Listing 10.3 Response Classification List

Visibility	Desirability	Prescriptive	Response Category
external	normal	binding	Normal
external	NSR	binding	NSR
external	error	binding	Error
internal	normal	binding	D&I Constraint, normal
internal	normal	guidance	D&I Guidance, normal
internal	error	binding	D&I Constraint, error
internal	error	guidance	D&I Guidance, error

10.3 Behavior Tables

A behavior table is a tabular notation that serves as a container for recording the total response behavior for all stimuli of a single stimulus set in a regular and systematic way. One rule and two guidelines govern the creation of behavior tables.

- Rule: One behavior table is created for each unique stimulus set of the functionality tree.
- Guideline 1: One column is created for each response classification list category.
- Guideline 2. One row is created for each stimulus of the stimulus set.

10.3.1 Behavior Table Rule and Format

Rule: One behavior table is created for each unique stimulus set of the functionality tree.

A requirements specification consists of one functionality tree and N behavior tables, where N is the number of unique stimulus sets in the functionality tree. In this context, "unique" means that one behavior table specifies the responses for all instances of a repetitive or reusable stimulus set. It makes no difference if the instances are in the same or different functionality trees (i.e., the same or different application programs); they share the same behavior table.

If the behavior needs to vary slightly for different instances, it can be regulated via input parameters. If the response differences are too severe to be configurable via behavior parameters, then the stimulus sets are not really repetitive due to substantial behavioral differences, even though the list of stimuli may appear to be the same. That apparently identical stimulus sets can really be different becomes clearer when one considers that a stimulus set is more properly a cohesive collection of requirements, where a requirement is not just a stimulus but a stimulus–response pair.

The general format of a behavior table is shown in Listing 10.4. The first line of the behavior table template specifies the name of the stimulus set to which the behavior table applies. Details regarding the rows and columns are discussed below. Notes may be appended below the table for clarification purposes.

Listing 10.4   Behavior Table Format Template

```
Behavior Table for <stimulus set name>
                                        D & I       D & I
Stimulus   Normal    NSR       Error    Constraint  Guidance   PAP
--------   --------  --------  -------- ----------  --------   --------
stim_name
--------   --------  --------  -------- ----------  --------   --------
   :
--------   --------  --------  -------- ----------  --------   --------
stim_name
--------   --------  --------  -------- ----------  --------   --------
```

10.3.2 Behavior Table Columns

> Guideline 1: One column is created for each response classification list category.

The leftmost (first) column of the behavior table template in Listing 10.4 lists each stimulus of the stimulus set. The second column records the normal response for each stimulus. The third column records the NSR for each stimulus, and the fourth records error response. The first four columns, plus any associated information in the PAP column (described below), comprise the complete external behavior and are therefore the only columns applicable to requirements specification.

In Listing 10.4, normal and error responses are merged for internal (Constraint and Guidance) responses because these are of less significance to requirements specification than external responses. These columns may be expanded to segregate normal and error internal responses if desired.

The fifth column is used to record any D&I constraints for the stimulus. Because D&I constraints are to be avoided, the fifth column will be blank unless the customer specifically requests particular internal response behavior. Any internal response behavior specified in the D&I column is just as binding on the development team as the true requirements. That is, the development team must implement the behavior specified in Column 5 exactly as specified.

The sixth column is used to record any optional D&I guidance that the customer or development team members wish to suggest. D&I guidance is internal responses that are nonbinding on the development team. Column 6 responses need not be implemented as specified, and need not even be implemented at all.

The last (rightmost) column contains optional performance, accuracy, and precision (PAP) requirements for the behavior specified in Columns 2 to 6. Performance refers to any applicable timing or periodicity requirements for the response. Accuracy refers to the permissible range of values that a quantity of the responses may take, including permissible deviations and tolerances. Precision refers to the number of significant digits that must be provided for a number, or the required data type of a quantity, such as integer or floating point. A PAP requirement should be horizontally aligned with the line of the response specification to which it applies, or annotated as necessary to clarify its scope. PAP column entries are binding on the development team to the same extent as the lines to which they apply. For example, a PAP entry that applies to an external response is a requirement, whereas one that applies to an entry in the Guidance column is simply D&I guidance.

10.3.3 Behavior Table Rows

Guideline 2. One row is created for each stimulus of the stimulus set.

As Listing 10.4 shows, each row of the behavior table specifies the response to one stimulus of the stimulus set. Rows are delineated by horizontal row separators for clarity, and to avoid ambiguity or errors that might result from a response specification "running on" into the row of the stimulus immediately below.

In addition to the stimuli specified in the stimulus set, an optional "initialization" stimulus may be added as the first row of a behavior table. The initialization stimulus records any externally visible behavior associated with activation of the stimulus set. For example, displaying a default value in a data stimulus input field on activation can be specified as part of the response to the initialization stimulus.

10.3.4 Behavior Table Generic Example

Listing 10.5 illustrates the correspondence between a functionality tree and its behavior tables. The generic functionality tree is the same one presented in Chapter 8. This functionality tree consists of four stimulus sets, one of which is repetitive, for a total of three unique stimulus sets. Therefore, three behavior tables are specified, one for each unique stimulus set of the functionality tree. Each behavior table contains a row for the initialization stimulus plus a row for each stimulus in its corresponding stimulus set. All the behavior tables contain the same columns, which correspond to the categories of the response classification list most relevant to requirements. The tables are empty: the cells remain to be filled in with response language statements specifying the required response behavior for each stimulus.

10.3.5 Behavior Table Benefits and Costs

Behavior tables ease response specification by making the process more regular, orderly, and systematic. The Rule ties behavior tables to the functionality tree in an orderly way that makes it easy to find the response specification for a given stimulus. The Rule and Guideline 2 together ensure that responses are specified for all stimuli, thus helping to ensure behavioral completeness of the requirements.

Guideline 1 makes the process of specifying the response to a single stimulus more systematic by explicitly breaking the total response down

Listing 10.5   Generic Functionality Tree and Behavior Tables

```
Level 0        Level 1        Level 2

SS 0-A         SS 1-A
stim 0-1       stim 1-1
                              SS 2-A
               stim 1-2       stim 2-1
                              stim 2-2
                              stim 2-3
                              stim 2-4
               SS 2-A
stim 0-2       (reused SS)

stim 0-3

------------------------------------------------------------------------

Behavior Table for SS 0-A
                                            D & I       D & I
Stimulus   Normal    NSR       Error        Constraint  Guidance   PAP
--------   -------   -------   --------      ----------  --------   --------
init
--------   -------   -------   --------      ----------  --------   --------
stim 0-1
--------   -------   -------   --------      ----------  --------   --------
stim 0-2
--------   -------   -------   --------      ----------  --------   --------
stim 0-3
--------   -------   -------   --------      ----------  --------   --------


------------------------------------------------------------------------

Behavior Table for SS 1-A
                                            D & I       D & I
Stimulus   Normal    NSR       Error        Constraint  Guidance   PAP
--------   -------   -------   --------      ----------  --------   --------
init
--------   -------   -------   --------      ----------  --------   --------
stim 1-1
--------   -------   -------   --------      ----------  --------   --------
stim 1-2
--------   -------   -------   --------      ----------  --------   --------


------------------------------------------------------------------------

Behavior Table for SS 2-A
                                            D & I       D & I
Stimulus   Normal    NSR       Error        Constraint  Guidance   PAP
--------   -------   -------   --------      ----------  --------   --------
init
--------   -------   -------   --------      ----------  --------   --------
stim 2-1
--------   -------   -------   --------      ----------  --------   --------
stim 2-2
--------   -------   -------   --------      ----------  --------   --------
stim 2-3
--------   -------   -------   --------      ----------  --------   --------
stim 2-4
--------   -------   -------   --------      ----------  --------   --------
```

into its constituent parts as defined by the response classification list. This helps to ensure that each response is complete, which also contributes to behavioral completeness of the requirements.

Ambiguity in the requirements specification is reduced by proper choice of a recording language, as discussed in Section 10.4.

Tools suitable for the creation of behavior tables must be capable of maintaining proper column alignment. Commodity tools such as spreadsheets and text editors that use fixed-pitch fonts are adequate, and low cost or even free. Spreadsheets have the advantage that column alignment is easy to maintain, and the amount of behavior specification text entered into each cell is not limited by the initial size of the cell. Text editors have the advantage that the resulting behavior table is stored in human-readable format, which is easier to e-mail or communicate to others who may have different software tools than the development team. Either way, from a tools standpoint, behavior tables can be developed easily and inexpensively.

Of course, the real work of developing behavior tables is specifying response behavior. This task may at first seem almost as onerous as programming (so why bother with behavior tables, just write the code!) but this is far from being the case. Two factors collude to make behavior specification far faster, easier, and simpler than coding.

The first, and most important, factor is that only external behavior is relevant to requirements specification. Any part of the response not detectable by a human user, external system, or the external environment need not, and should not, be specified. Focusing only on the external response, and deliberately ignoring how it is achieved internally, vastly simplifies behavior specification, vastly reduces the time and effort involved, and, happily, creates a proper requirements specification unpolluted by gratuitous D&I information.

The second simplifying factor is that, as with the other three aspects of requirements,[4] behavior specification is performed with the help of customer staff or their POC. A behavior table is best created by a team of two: the POC who verbally dictates what the external response to each stimulus should be, and a developer who creates the table as the POC dictates. This approach, which is akin to pair programming, is called "pair specification." Pair specification is a highly effective and efficient way to specify and record required behavior in behavior tables.

As a result of external focus and pair specification, behavior specification should not exceed ten percent of the effort of coding,[5] and most of this is recouped by reduced coding effort, resulting in little net cost to the project. If behavior specification exceeds ten percent, it is probably being done incorrectly.

10.4 Response Recording Languages

An ideal language for recording response behavior would

- Be easy to read for customers
- Segregate external and internal behavior
- Be cost-effective to use
- Be clear and unambiguous
- Be easy to write for developers
- Reduce "conceptual distance" from requirements to implementation
- Be easy to process automatically into programming code

In practice, there are three language types suitable for behavior recording: natural language (prose), formal methods, and program design language (PDL). Table 10.1 is a comparison of these three alternatives relative to the above needs of response recording.

Natural language prose is widely used for requirements specification due to being highly readable and writeable. However, prose lacks rigor, has ambiguous semantics, and, consequently, is very difficult to process automatically. Worse, it offers no facilities for segregating external information (requirements) from internal information (D&I). Prose has a reasonable cost of creation, but its shortcomings tend to escalate costs downstream in the development process.

Table 10.1   Response Recording Notation Comparison

Rank	Attribute	Actor Served	FM	Prose	PDL
1	Readability	Customer	Poor	**Good**	Fair
2	External focus	Customer	**Good**	Poor	**Good**[a]
3	Cost of use	Customer	Poor	Fair	**Good**
4	Writeability	Developer	Poor	Fair	**Good**
5	Unambiguous	Developer	**Good**	Poor	Fair
6	"Conceptual distance" to code	Developer	**Good**	Poor	Fair
7	Automation	Developer	**Good**	Poor	Fair

[a] Freedom variant, when combined with behavior table.

Formal methods are rigorous, unambiguous, easily automated notations, the best known and most successful of which are programming languages. Because computers only understand a formal method called machine code, requirements expressed in natural language or PDL must, at some point, be converted to a formal method for autotranslation to machine code. Programming languages effect this natural-to-machine language conversion manually during implementation. To date, formal methods for requirements and external behavior specification have failed due to being unreadable by customers, "painful" to use for developers,[6] and costing as much to use as a programming language while not eliminating programming.

PDL, sometimes called "structured English," is nearly as readable as prose, and is perhaps easier because most rules of grammar are suspended in PDL. Consequently, the cost of use is low. Although not anywhere near as rigorous as a formal method, PDL's use of some structured constructs permits some automation to be easily performed. Structure also helps reduce ambiguity, especially with respect to logic.

As Table 10.1 shows, PDL, although far from being ideal, is a good compromise between natural language prose and formal methods. That PDL is a good compromise is further demonstrated by the fact that *nobody* likes PDL: as every politician knows, this is a sure sign of a good compromise! The fact that no one will ever be happy with PDL also ensures that its use will never impede the search for something better. Hence, Freedom currently uses PDL for behavior recording.

10.5 Response Recording Syntax

The deficiencies of common PDL for required behavior capture are well known.[7] These deficiencies include poor support for automatic syntax checking and code generation, and a propensity to record internal behavior (D&I) in addition to external behavior (requirements).[8] The variant of PDL recommended for use with Freedom partially alleviates these problems by the simple expedient of explicitly declaring input, output, and local quantities. Explicit quantity declaration improves support for automated consistency and error checking. This, and placing the PDL in the context of behavior tables, improves support for automatic generation of code such as class, method, and field variable declarations. As we show later, explicit quantity declaration also helps in segregating external from internal behavior.

The complete syntax of the PDL variant recommended for use with Freedom is given in Listing 10.6. The following subsections explain the syntax in more detail.

Listing 10.6   Recommended PDL Syntax

```
A. Declaration statements
   Input
      input_quantity
        :

   Output
      output_quantity
        :

   Local
      temp_quantity
        :

   Body
      sequence, selection, repetition statements

B. Sequence statement
   operation on declared quantity (phrase)

C. Selection statement
   IF condition
   THEN
      sequence, selection, repetition statements
[ ELSE
      sequence, selection, repetition statements ]
   END IF

D. Repetition statement
   DO { WHILE | FOR } condition
      sequence, selection, repetition statements
   END DO
```

10.5.1 Declaration Statements

Syntax

```
Input
   input_quantity
     :
```

Example

```
Input
   speed_of_travel
   time_traveled
```

Input is a keyword that indicates a list of input quantities follows. Quantity names are natural language and need not follow any rigorous syntax, except that they must be used consistently (including spelling) throughout the PDL once declared. Each quantity name should appear on a separate line to promote unambiguous association with any PAP column requirements. Although not required, joining the different words of a quantity name with an underscore or hyphen can reduce ambiguity and improve readability of the PDL. For example:

```
first_name      NOT   first name
middle_initial  NOT   middle initial
last_name       NOT   last name
```

A name should describe or otherwise identify the quantity as clearly and unambiguously as possible. The Input keyword should be the first PDL statement of a response description. It may be omitted if the response to the stimulus has no input data.

Syntax

```
Output
    output_quantity
       :
```

Example

```
Output
    distance_traveled
    error_message
```

Output is a keyword that indicates a list of output quantities follows. The guidelines are the same as for Input quantities above. The Output keyword must follow the Input keyword, if it exists. Otherwise, the Output keyword will be the first PDL statement of a response description. It may be omitted if the response to the stimulus has no output data.

Syntax

```
Local
    temp_quantity
       :
```

Example

```
Local
    ft-meters_conv_factor
```

Local is a keyword that indicates a list of temporary or local (i.e., noninput/output) quantities follows. The guidelines are the same as for Input quantities above. The Local keyword must follow the Input and Output keywords, if any. Otherwise, the Local keyword will be the first PDL statement of a response description. The Local keyword may be omitted if the response to the stimulus needs no temporary data.

Quantities declared under a Local declaration are for use by internal responses (D&I Constraints and Guidance) only. External responses (Normal, NSR, and Error) should not use Local quantities.

Syntax

```
Body
    sequence, selection, repetition statements
```

Example

```
Body
    compute distance_traveled
    display distance_traveled
```

Body is a keyword that indicates the main body of the behavior PDL follows. Any combination of sequence, selection, and repetition statements may follow the Body keyword. At least one such statement is required, as is the Body keyword. The Body keyword must follow the Input, Output, and Local keywords, if they exist. Otherwise, the Body keyword will be the first PDL statement of a response description.

10.5.2 *Sequence Statement*

Syntax

```
operation on declared quantity (phrase)
```

Example

```
compute distance_traveled
display distance_traveled
```

A sequence statement is a phrase that unambiguously specifies an action or operation on a declared quantity. Sequence statements should be as short as possible, consistent with clarity. Complete sentences and pronouns should be avoided. Each sequence statement must be on its own line to promote unambiguous association with any PAP column requirements. Any quantity mentioned in a sequence statement must be declared in an Input, Output, or Local list. Operations on the quantities need not be formally declared.

10.5.3 Selection Statement

Syntax

```
IF condition
THEN
    sequence, selection, repetition statements
[ ELSE
    sequence, selection, repetition statements ]
END IF
```

Example

```
IF speed_of_travel or
    time_traveled is negative
THEN
    display error_message
ELSE
    compute distance_traveled
    display distance_traveled
END IF
```

A selection statement permits behavior to vary based on a logical condition. Any quantity mentioned in the condition of the IF must be declared in an Input, Output, or Local list. Operations on the quantities need not be formally declared. Any number and combination of sequence, selection, and repetition statements may follow the THEN and ELSE keywords. The behavior following THEN is performed if the condition is true; otherwise, the behavior following the ELSE is performed. The ELSE keyword and its associated sequence, selection, and repetition statements are optional, as indicated by the square brackets [ ]. If the condition is false and no ELSE behavior is specified, the null response is assumed. The selection statement is terminated by the END IF keyword.

10.5.4 *Repetition Statement*

Syntax

```
DO { WHILE | FOR }  condition
   sequence, selection, repetition statements
END DO
```

Example

```
DO WHILE speed_of_travel is positive
   compute distance_traveled
   display distance_traveled
   decrement speed_of_travel by 1.0 km/hr
END DO
```

A repetition statement permits behavior to repeat based on a logical condition. Either the WHILE or FOR keyword must follow the DO keyword. If a WHILE is present, the behavior repeats as long as the condition is true. If a FOR is present, the condition is counter logic and the behavior repeats the number of times specified by the counter logic. Any quantity mentioned in the condition must be declared in an Input, Output, or Local list. Operations on the quantities need not be formally declared. Any number and combination of sequence, selection, and repetition statements specifying the behavior to be repeated may follow the DO WHILE or DO FOR keywords. The repetition statement is terminated by the END DO keyword.

10.6 Example Problem Behavior Tables

With stimuli identified and organized into a functionality tree, the Furmasco inventory system development team is ready to start defining responses to those stimuli. They start by organizing the team into pairs, with each pair consisting of one team member from IT and one from shipping. The pair assigned to human interface response specification agrees that the shipping department person will act as the customer and have primary responsibility for behavior specification inasmuch as shipping will be the primary users of the human user interface. The pair assigned to the programmatic interface to the app server decides the IT team member should play the customer role because the IT app server system will be the user of the inventory programmatic interface.

Let's listen in on the "pair specification" team for the human interface.

10.6.1 Example Problem Human Interface Behavior Tables

IT: Let's start by creating empty behavior tables for all of our stimulus sets. Then we will be ready to write down behavior for any stimulus anytime.

Shipping: Good idea. The functionality tree says we need four tables, one each for Classif SS, Mode SS, Furniture List SS, and Furniture Data SS. Should we create a different file for each table, or put all the tables in one file? With one file, we would not have to keep opening and closing files whenever we make a change.

IT: We can avoid that by keeping all the files open at once, and iconizing them when not in use. One file per table will make things like printing a single table easier.

Shipping: What do the quality requirements say to do?

IT: The only quality requirement that applies here is maintainability. I have found that code is easier to maintain when each class is in its own file. I think placing each table in its own file will be easier to maintain, too. Let's see what the other team is doing.

They check with the programmatic interface team. Together, the teams agree to put each behavior table in its own file for better maintainability, and for consistency with the code inasmuch as the code will be stored one functionality module per file (see Chapter 12). The human interface team then creates their tables by cutting and pasting a template like that of Listing 10.4 into four separate files. They then type the name of a stimulus set into the header of each table, and create a table row for each stimulus of the stimulus set plus a row for the initialization stimulus. Each file is named after the stimulus set, with a ".bt" (behavior table) extension added.

Shipping: The first stimulus set is Classif SS, so let's start there.

They discuss the externally visible response that should occur when the inventory system is first started. As shipping verbalizes their conclusions in short phrases, IT enters the behavior into the table. Their results are shown in Listings 10.7 through 10.11. Some of their discussions may be worth recounting in detail.

*   *   *

Listing 10.7 Inventory Human Interface "Classification" Behavior Table

```
Behavior Table for Inventory Human User Classification SS
                                     D & I       D & I
Stimulus  Normal    NSR      Error   Constraint  Guidance  PAP
--------  --------  -------- -------- ----------  --------  --------
init      Input
            list_of_categories
          Body
                    enable list_of_categories stimuli
                    clear list_of_types stimuli
--------  --------  -------- -------- ----------  --------  --------
list of categ
          Input
            list_of_types
          Output
            selected_category
          Body
          highlight selected_category
                    display list_of_types for selected_category
                    clear Furniture List SS stimuli
--------  --------  -------- -------- ----------  --------  --------
list of types
          Output
            selected_type
          Body
          highlight selected_type
                    activate Furniture List SS for selected_type
--------  --------  -------- -------- ----------  --------  --------
```

IT: Now that we have all of our (empty) behavior tables, let's fill them in starting with the NSR behavior shown in the functionality tree. That way we can be sure the behavior tables match the tree.

Shipping reads the NSR responses from the functionality tree while IT enters them into the behavior tables.

Shipping: Classif SS "list of types" stimulus activates Furn List SS.

IT: list of types: activate [*typing sounds*] Furniture List SS [*typing sounds*]. OK.

. . . and so on for each NSR response in the functionality tree. When they are done, IT reads back the NSR responses from the table while shipping verifies they match the functionality tree. Everything checks.

Listing 10.8 Inventory Human Interface "Mode" Behavior Table

```
Behavior Table for Inventory Human User Mode SS
                                       D & I       D & I
Stimulus   Normal     NSR      Error   Constraint  Guidance  PAP
--------   --------   -------- -------- ----------  --------  --------
init       Body
           perform view response
--------   --------   -------- -------- ----------  --------  --------
view       Body
           mark view stimulus as selected
           unmark add, modify stimuli
                   disable Furniture Data SS for input
--------   --------   -------- -------- ----------  --------  --------
add        Body
           mark add stimulus as selected
           unmark view, modify stimuli
                   enable Furniture Data SS stimuli for input
--------   --------   -------- -------- ----------  --------  --------
modify     Body
           mark modify stimulus as selected
           unmark view, add stimuli
                   enable Furniture Data SS quantity, price,
                   select, reset for input
                   disable Furniture Data SS descrip, shipping wt,
                   dimensions for input
--------   --------   -------- -------- ----------  --------  --------
```

IT: You know, it should be possible to automate everything we have done up to now. A program could read in the functionality tree and write out empty behavior tables for each stimulus set, except with the NSR responses already filled in. In principle, it shouldn't be too hard to do.

Shipping: Why don't you IT guys go do it?

IT: Yeah, like our Furmasco CFO is going to pay for it! Actually, it would be interesting to come up with a programmatic functionality tree for reading a functionality tree. That's how you'd have to start—by figuring out how a functionality tree breaks into stimuli, and how those stimuli organize into stimulus sets and a functionality tree.

Shipping: Sort of like a functionality tree for functionality trees?

IT: Exactly!

Shipping: Sounds challenging. The input functionality tree would be all data stimuli. Where are the command stimuli to help with figuring out the levels?

Listing 10.9   Inventory Human Interface "Furniture List" Behavior Table

```
Behavior Table for Inventory Human User Furniture List SS
                                         D & I       D & I
Stimulus   Normal    NSR       Error     Constraint  Guidance  PAP
--------   --------  --------  --------  ----------  --------  --------
init       Input
             selected_type
             list_of_furniture
           Body
           IF selected_type is set
           THEN
                    clear list_of_furn stimuli
                    display list_of_furniture for selected_type as
                      new list_of_furn stimuli
           END IF
--------   --------  --------  --------  ----------  --------  --------
list of furniture
           Input
             descrip
             quantity
             price
             shipping wt
             dimensions
           Output
             selected_furn_item
           Body
           highlight selected_furn_item
           display descrip, quantity, price, shipping wt, dimensions
             for selected_furn_item in Furniture Data SS
--------   --------  --------  --------  ----------  --------  --------
```

IT: Well, data stimuli can activate stimulus sets, too. Command stimuli are not absolutely necessary. But you are right; they do help, a lot. That's why it might be easier to first create an XML structure for storing a functionality tree. The XML tags then become the command stimuli, and the stimulus sets and functionality tree should just fall right out of the XML tag levels. A functionality tree is a really simple data structure. It would not be very hard to create an XML tag set for it.

Shipping: You make it sound so easy! Well, I guess that's why you're in IT and I'm in shipping. Speaking of which. . .

IT: Yeah—back to the inventory program.

*   *   *

Listing 10.10   Inventory Human Interface "Furniture Data" Behavior Table

```
Behavior Table for Inventory Human User Furniture Data SS (1 of 3)
                                       D & I       D & I
Stimulus  Normal    NSR       Error    Constraint  Guidance  PAP
--------  --------  --------  --------  ----------  --------  --------
init      Body
                    disable all stimuli of this SS for input
          clear descrip, quantity, price, shipping wt, dimensions
--------  --------  --------  --------  ----------  --------  --------
description
          Input
            description                                       string
          Body
          echo description
--------  --------  --------  --------  ----------  --------  --------
quantity  Input
            quantity                                          integer
          Body
          echo quantity
          clear message area
          IF quantity not integral
          THEN
                         display error message in message area
                         display original quantity
          ELSE IF quantity is negative
          THEN
            display 'negative quantity deletes item' message
              in message area
          END IF
--------  --------  --------  --------  ----------  --------  --------
price     Input
            price                                             $ US
          Body
          echo price
          clear message area
          IF price is not a number or
            price is negative or zero
          THEN
                         display error message in message area
                         display original price
          END IF
--------  --------  --------  --------  ----------  --------  --------
shipping wt
          Input
            shipping wt                                       lbs.
          Body
          echo shipping wt
          clear message area
          IF shipping wt is not a number or
            shipping wt is negative
          THEN
                         display error message in message area
                         display original shipping wt
          END IF
--------  --------  --------  --------  ----------  --------  --------
```

**Listing 10.10   Inventory Human Interface "Furniture Data"
Behavior Table (continued)**

```
----------------------------------------------------------------------
Behavior Table for Inventory Human User Furniture Data SS (2 of 3)
                                         D & I       D & I
Stimulus  Normal    NSR      Error    Constraint Guidance  PAP
--------  --------  --------  --------  ----------  --------  --------
dimensions
          Input
              dimensions (w,h,d)                              inches
          Body
          echo dimensions
          clear message area
          IF dimensions not comma separated string of 3 values or
             values are not all numbers or
             values are not all positive
          THEN
                          display error message in message area
                          display original dimensions
          END IF
--------  --------  --------  --------  ----------  --------  --------
select    Input
              list_of_furniture
          Output
            descrip
            quantity
            price
            shipping wt
            dimensions
          Local
            inventory
          Body
          clear message area
          IF any data field is blank
                          display error message in message area
          ELSE IF quantity is negative
                              delete descrip item from
                                  inventory
                  remove descrip item from list_of_furniture
                  in Furniture List SS
            display 'item deleted' message in message area
          ELSE
                              update descrip item in
                                  inventory
                              with quantity, price,
                              shipping wt, dimensions
            display 'item saved' message in message area
          END IF
--------  --------  --------  --------  ----------  --------  --------
```

Listing 10.10 Inventory Human Interface "Furniture Data" Behavior Table (continued)

```
---------------------------------------------------------------------
Behavior Table for Inventory Human User Furniture Data SS (3 of 3)
                                         D & I       D & I
Stimulus  Normal    NSR        Error     Constraint  Guidance  PAP
--------  --------  --------   --------   ----------  --------  --------
reset     Input
             selected_furn_item
             descrip
             quantity
             price
             shipping wt
             dimensions
          Body
          IF selected_furn_item is set
             set descrip, quantity, price, shipping wt, dimensions
              in Furniture Data SS from selected_furn_item
          ELSE
             clear descrip, quantity, price, shipping wt, dimensions in
              Furniture Data SSS
          END IF
--------  --------  --------   --------   ----------  --------  --------
```

Listing 10.11   Inventory Human Interface "Inventory" Behavior Table

```
Behavior Table for Inventory Human User Inventory SS
                                         D & I       D & I
Stimulus  Normal    NSR        Error     Constraint  Guidance  PAP
--------  --------  --------   --------   ----------  --------  --------
init      Body
          display human interface screen
                      activate Mode SS
                      activate Classification SS
--------  --------  --------   --------   ----------  --------  --------
quit      Body
                      exit program
--------  --------  --------   --------   ----------  --------  --------
```

Shipping: The Classif SS "init" stimulus should also activate the Level 0 programmatic Cmd Type SS.

IT: init: activate [*typing sounds*] Cmd Type SS [*typing sounds*]. Got it. . . . Hmm. Should our human interface activate the programmatic interface, or should it activate us? Or should each interface be a separate program activated independently of the operating system?

Shipping: Time for the quality requirements!

IT: Right.

Table 10.2   Inventory System Level 0 SS Activation Trade-Off

Rank	Quality Attribute	Human Activates Programmatic	Programmatic Activates Human	Both Activated Independently
1	Functionality	Harder to support multiple human UIs	Harder to support multiple human UIs	**Easier to support multiple human UIs over LAN per context diagram**
2	Reliability	Possible conflict among multiple progr. instances	Possible conflict among multiple progr. instances	**Only one progr. interface instance**
3	Maintainability	No significant difference	No significant difference	No significant difference
4	Usability	*N* human UI instances create *N* progr. instances	Must run *N* progr. instances to run *N* human UIs	**One progr. instance for N human UI instances**
5	Administerability	User starts both processes	Sys. Admin. starts both processes	**Sys. Ad. starts progr. process, users start UI processes**
6	Execution Speed	Slower: both always running	Slower: both always running	**Faster: if only one running**
7	Storage Demand	More: both always use resources	More: both always use resources	**Less: use only what is needed**

They analyze the three alternatives using the project's quality requirements. Their trade-off results, which are summarized in Table 10.2, are shown to the programmatic behavior team. The programmatic team agrees that the two types of interfaces should be launched separately as two different main programs. This decision effectively breaks the one logical inventory system black box into two physical black boxes for implementation.

The human interface team deletes the "activate Cmd Type SS" statement from the Classif SS "init" response.

*   *   *

Shipping: Next is the "list of categ" stimulus of the Classif SS stimulus set. Let's see—what happens when a user selects one of the categories, like "living room furniture?" The response should be "display list of types for selected category." The types would be furniture found in living rooms, like chairs, tables, and sofas.

IT: list of categ stimulus: display [*typing*] list of types for selected category [*typing*]. OK. Anything else? How about highlighting the selected category so the user knows which one the mouse really hit?

Shipping: Of course—highlight selected category.

IT: highlight [*typing*] . . . Are any other parts of the screen affected?

Shipping: Well, the list of furniture in Furniture List SS is out of date now because the list of types has changed. So we should clear the list of furniture until a new "types" entry is selected.

IT: clear [*typing*] Furniture List SS [*typing*].

Shipping: How will the program know what the different furniture types for each category are? And the list of categories, too? I mean, everyone in shipping knows these categories and types by heart; they haven't changed in ages. But how do we tell the program? Do we just hard-nail them in?

IT: That's one way. Are you sure these categories and types will never change?

Shipping: Well, maybe not "never." There has been some talk about expanding into pool and deck furniture. If that happens, there will be a new category and a new set of types to go with it. Last time something like that happened was back in the '90s when we started building computer furniture. So I guess the categories and types do change, but not very often.

IT: Then the choice is between hard-nailing them and reading the categories from a simple configuration file that can be maintained manually. Either way, we can just edit the source file or configuration file by hand on the rare occasions when a new category needs to be added.

Shipping: If we read the classification categories from a file, then we need to create a programmatic protocol functionality tree for the file format, right?

IT: In other words, do we need to add the data classification input file to the requirements? It depends. Will the users or the app server need to know about the classification file?

Shipping: Probably not. They will only see the classification categories through the inventory system interface. I don't think anyone except the inventory system will need to get to the file directly.

IT: Good. Because the file would be internal to the inventory system, it is not part of the requirements information. We can worry about its interface when we get to design. If we decide to use a file, we can develop a functionality tree for it then, or use a pre-existing protocol such as the JReality data classification package. In that case, we would not need to develop a functionality tree or custom protocol code at all. Hard-nailing the classification categories into the code would eliminate the need to invent a new protocol too. Hard-nailing isn't flexible but is a simple approach when things don't change that often, and code redistribution is not a major issue.

Shipping: Sounds like you favor hard-nailing.

IT: The simplest way that works is usually the best.

Shipping: Well, I said to hard-nail the categories in the first place.

IT: Lucky guess!

Shipping: No, man. Just smart!

IT: Sure. Let's get back to work.

*   *   *

Shipping: We're getting near the end! Next is Furniture Data SS "dimensions" stimulus. The normal response should be to just echo the dimensions input.

IT: echo dimensions [*typing*]. Any error response?

Shipping: All three values must be positive. We have yet to invent furniture that takes up zero or negative space!

IT: No high-tech start-ups in the furniture industry, eh? OK. IF values [*typing*] not all positive THEN [*typing*]. What, display an error message?

Shipping: Right. And then restore the original values. Don't want bad values getting into the database by accident.

IT: display error message [*typing*]. The user is entering the three dimensions as one comma-separated list, right?

Shipping: Right.

IT: Sounds like that could be confusing. What if they mix up the numbers—get them in the wrong order, or leave one out? Wouldn't a separate data stimulus for each dimension be better?

Shipping: I asked our shipping data entry clerks about that. They said they are used to entering the three values as a comma-separated list in the old system, and would rather we just keep it that way. Said it would just slow them down to deal with three entry fields instead of just one. They're used to doing it the old way.

IT: OK—it's your system! In any case, if your clerks ever change their minds, it shouldn't be hard to modify the code. This Freedom approach makes interface changes like that a lot easier. Just don't tell them I said so!

Shipping: Yeah, then they'll ask for changes every five minutes! It will be our secret.

*　　　*　　　*

The pair specification team working on the behavior tables for the programmatic interface proceeds in a similar manner. Because the IT app server is the user of the programmatic interface, the IT team member dictates the required behavior while the team member from shipping types into the behavior table. Their results are shown in Listings 10.12 through 10.16.

10.6.2 Behavior Specification in Reality

The above examples of the behavior specification process are idealistic: the Furmasco "pair specification" teams nearly always made the right decisions on the first try. In reality, it never works that way. The actual process of creating development work products is considerably messier.

For example, when specifying the programmatic protocol functionality tree, the author originally had the Furn Data SS stimulus set at Level 2, activated by stimulus 10 at the same time that Descrip SS was activated:

```
Cmd Type SS    Descrip SS
10             description

               Furn Data SS
               12
               etc.
```

This looked reasonable at first. However, when creating the behavior table for Descrip SS, deeper thought into the behavior made it apparent that Furn Data SS should be activated by the Descrip SS stimulus, not by stimulus 10 of Cmd Data SS. This necessitated a revision of the programmatic interface functionality tree as well as of the previously specified behavior for stimulus 10:

```
Cmd Type SS    Descrip SS     Furn Data SS
10             description     12
                               etc.
```

This is representative of the iteration among notations that takes place when specifying requirements using the black box stimulus–response model. Behavior specification provides deeper understanding of the requirements, and in so doing helps refine the stimuli and their organization (which is why behavior specification precedes requirements prioritization in the "rational" process of Figure 10.1). The final work products should mask the messiness and make it look as if the rational process was followed without a hitch. This is what Parnas and Clements called "faking it."[9]

Listing 10.12   Inventory Programatic Interface "Cmd Type" Behavior Table

```
Behavior Table for Inventory Programatic Cmd Type SS
                                        D & I      D & I
Stimulus  Normal    NSR       Error     Constraint Guidance  PAP
--------  --------  --------  --------  ---------- --------  --------
init      Body
                    enable all stimuli of this SS
--------  --------  --------  --------  ---------- --------  --------
01        Body
                    disable all stimuli of this SS
                    activate Categ SS
--------  --------  --------  --------  ---------- --------  --------
02        Body
                    disable all stimuli of this SS
                    activate Type SS
--------  --------  --------  --------  ---------- --------  --------
03        Input
            category
            type
            descrip_list
            inventory_items
          Body
          IF category is set in Categ SS and
             type is set in Type SS
          THEN
             send descrip_List for all inventory_items
             matching category and type
          END IF
--------  --------  --------  --------  ---------- --------  --------
10        Body
                    disable all stimuli of this SS
                    activate Descrip SS
--------  --------  --------  --------  ---------- --------  --------
```

There is a lot of "faking" the rational process due to iteration among functionality tree, functionality screens, protocol specs, and behavior tables. Most of the insight that leads to this iteration is gleaned during creation of the behavior tables. Behavior table creation is much faster and easier than might be expected (and with pair specification can even be fun!), and the insight and iterative adjustments that result translate to much time, effort, and cost saved downstream. Behavior tables are a "pay me (a little) now or pay me (a lot more) later" proposition.

Never skip or skimp on the behavior tables!

Listing 10.13 Inventory Programatic Interface "Furn Data" Behavior Table

```
Behavior Table for Inventory Programatic Furn Data SS
                                     D & I        D & I
Stimulus  Normal     NSR      Error  Constraint  Guidance  PAP
--------  --------   --------  ------ ----------  --------  --------
init      Input
            description
          Body
          IF description is set in Descrip SS
          THEN
                    enable all stimuli of this SS
          ELSE
            perform 19 response
          END IF
--------  --------   --------  ------ ----------  --------  --------
12        Input
            quantity
            inventory_item
          Body
          send quantity for description inventory_item
--------  --------   --------  ------ ----------  --------  --------
13        Input
            price
            inventory_item
          Body
          send price for description inventory_item
--------  --------   --------  ------ ----------  --------  --------
14        Input
            shipping_wt
            inventory_item
          Body
          send shipping_wt for description inventory_item
--------  --------   --------  ------ ----------  --------  --------
15        Input
            dimensions                                      w,h,d
            inventory_item
          Body
          send dimensions for description inventory_item
--------  --------   --------  ------ ----------  --------  --------
19        Body
                     disable all stimuli of this SS
                     enable all stimuli of Cmd Type SS
--------  --------   --------  ------ ----------  --------  --------
```

Listing 10.14   Inventory Programatic Interface "Categ" Behavior Table

```
Behavior Table for Inventory Programatic Categ SS
                                     D & I        D & I
Stimulus  Normal    NSR       Error  Constraint  Guidance   PAP
--------  --------  --------  --------  ----------  --------  --------
init      Body
                    enable all stimuli of this SS

--------  --------  --------  --------  ----------  --------  --------
categ     Input
            category                                           string
          Body
                                        save category
                    disable all stimuli of this SS
                    enable all stimuli of Cmd Type SS
--------  --------  --------  --------  ----------  --------  --------
```

Listing 10.15   Inventory Programatic Interface "Type" Behavior Table

```
Behavior Table for Inventory Programatic Type SS
                                     D & I        D & I
Stimulus  Normal    NSR       Error  Constraint  Guidance   PAP
--------  --------  --------  --------  ----------  --------  --------
init      Input
            category
          Body
          IF category is set
          THEN
                    enable all stimuli of this SS
          ELSE
                    disable all stimuli of this SS
                    enable all stimuli of Cmd Type SS
          END IF
--------  --------  --------  --------  ----------  --------  --------
type      Input
            category
            type
          Body
          IF category is set in Categ SS and
             type is consistent with category
                                        save type
          END IF
                    disable all stimuli of this SS
                    enable all stimuli of Cmd Type SS
--------  --------  --------  --------  ----------  --------  --------
```

Listing 10.16   Inventory Programatic Interface "Descrip" Behavior Table

```
Behavior Table for Inventory Programatic Descrip SS
                                       D & I       D & I
Stimulus   Normal     NSR       Error  Constraint  Guidance  PAP
--------   --------   --------   --------   ----------   --------   --------
init       Body
                      enable all stimuli of this SS
--------   --------   --------   --------   ----------   --------   --------
description
           Input
              description                                          string
           Body
                                      save description
                      disable all stimuli of this SS
                      enable all stimuli of Furn Data SS
--------   --------   --------   --------   ----------   --------   --------
```

References

1. A response that originates with a module and is sent to an external destination is considered an external response to the external stimulus that triggered execution of the module.
2. Lutowski, R. 1978. Classification lists—A useful way to organize ship design data. *Naval Engineers Journal* (December), pages 87–94.
3. Warfield, J. 1983. Organizations and systems learning. In Proceedings of the *27th Annual Meeting of the Society for General Systems Research*, Detroit, MI, May, Appendix 6.
4. Stimulus identification, protocol specification, and mockup prototyping.
5. Berry, D.M. 2002. Formal methods: The very idea, some thoughts about why they work when they work. *Science of Computer Programming* 42: 1 (January), Figure 2.
6. Berry, D.M. 2002. The inevitable pain of software development: Why there is no silver bullet. In *Proceedings of Monterey Workshop 2002, Radical Innovations of Software and Systems Engineering in the Future*, Venice, Italy, October, pages 28–47.
7. Davis, A.M. 1988. A comparison of techniques for the specification of external system behavior. *Communications of the ACM* 31: 9 (September), pages 1098–1115.
8. Formal method researchers are well aware of the distinction between external and internal behavior, and frequently strive to develop formal methods for requirements that specify only external behavior. Thus, formal method researchers have assumed the black box definition of requirements for decades, but have never made the assumption explicit per the Freedom definition.
9. Parnas, D.L. and Clements, P.C. 1986. A rational design process: How and why to fake it. *IEEE Transactions on Software Engineering* SE-12: 2 (February), pages 251–257.

Chapter 11

Requirements Encapsulation Design

11.1 Chapter Overview

The prioritized functionality tree and associated behavior tables should be reviewed for correctness and completeness by the intended users of the system. There are at least two ways to do this.

1. Hold a requirements review at which users examine the work products directly.
2. Construct an interface mockup prototype for evaluation use by the users.

A requirements review can be a viable approach on some projects, but a prototype is an effective approach in nearly all cases. Even on projects where requirements reviews can be held, a mockup prototype should also be used to obtain requirements feedback, as illustrated in Figure 11.1.

This chapter discusses the design, or gray box, concepts prerequisite to construction of the interface mockup. The first of these concepts is the requirements encapsulation design rule that maps the requirements to requirements encapsulating "functionality modules." The second concept is the "canonical design architecture," a universally applicable design architecture that follows naturally from encapsulation of requirements. Producing the prototype involves design and implementation of the functionality module portion of the canonical design architecture.

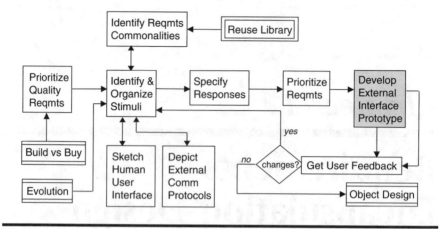

Figure 11.1   Functionality module architecture in the requirements process.

Create one functionality module for each
unique stimulus set in the functionality tree

Figure 11.2   Requirements encapsulation rule.

This chapter is not a comprehensive exposition of the Freedom design process, which is outside the scope of this book. This chapter is concerned only with those aspects of design relevant to creation of an external interface prototype suitable for user verification of the requirements.

11.2 Requirements Encapsulation Design Rule

A simple Freedom design rule relates requirements to their implementing modules. This rule, stated in Figure 11.2, is similar to the rule given in Chapter 10 for creating behavior tables, except "functionality module" replaces "behavior table." A functionality module (see Chapter 12) is a code module that implements and encapsulates the requirements of one stimulus set. The term "unique" in the rule means that repetitive or reusable stimulus sets require only a single functionality module, not one per repetition.

To illustrate application of the design rule, consider the generic functionality tree from Chapter 9, which is replicated at the top of Figure 11.3. This functionality tree contains three unique stimulus sets: SS 0 – A, SS 1 – A, and SS 2 – A. Because there are three unique stimulus sets, the

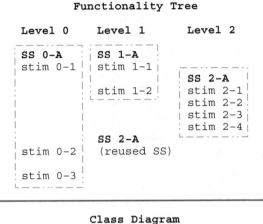

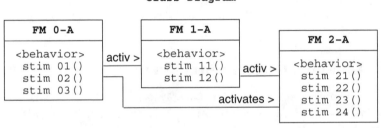

Figure 11.3 Design rule applied to generic functionality tree.

requirements encapsulation design rule specifies that three functionality modules be created, one for each stimulus set. As shown at the bottom of Figure 11.3, the functionality module (FM) that implements SS 0 – A encapsulates three requirements, namely, the stimulus–response pairs for stim 0 – 1, stim 0 – 2, and stim 0 – 3. The functionality module that implements SS 1 – A encapsulates the two stimulus–response pairs of SS 1 – A. The functionality module that implements SS 2 – A encapsulates the four requirements of the repetitive stimulus set SS 2 – A.

It is evident from the above that requirements traceability is not 1:1 but 1:N, where N is the number of stimulus–response pairs in the stimulus set. However, each stimulus–response pair (requirement) is encapsulated wholly within a single module. The 1:N mapping is superior to a 1:1 mapping because:

■ A 1:N mapping promulgates the strong cohesion of the stimulus sets in the code, resulting in highly cohesive functionality modules.
■ A 1:N mapping avoids the excessively large number of functionality modules that would result from a 1:1 mapping, with subsequent reduction in maintenance effort.

A module that implements a stimulus set must implement the NSR responses of its stimuli. As a result, the association relationship among the modules exactly mirrors the NSR relationship among the stimulus sets in the functionality tree. Thus, another effect of the design rule is to ensure that the design architecture of the functionality modules is identical to the requirements architecture; that is, requirements specification and requirements implementation are architecturally equivalent.

The architectural symmetry between requirements and design in Freedom makes development and maintenance easier. Once the requirements architecture (inherent in the functionality tree) is created, the architecture of the implementing design is also known (i.e., the requirements architecture serves a dual purpose). When a change is made to the requirements architecture, no additional work is necessary to know the impact on the design architecture. The architectural symmetry between requirements and design benefits initial development as well as subsequent maintenance.

11.3 Canonical Design Architecture

Although requirements in Freedom are design neutral, encapsulating them in objects assumes an OO design. An OO design that encapsulates requirements will always be canonical (i.e., universally invariant) in important ways. This canonical architecture is seen by peeling back the surface of the black box to reveal the gray box view of the system. The gray box view consists of canonical internal black boxes organized in a canonical way, as follows.

Each internal black box represents a code module that encapsulates a specific type of information that has a high probability of change. As described in Chapter 2, there are three major types of information that have a high probability of change: requirements (system external interfaces), design decisions, and interfaces to hardware.

Three module types correspond to the three types of encapsulated information, as summarized in Table 11.1. These are requirements encapsulation modules, design decision-hiding modules, and hardware interface-

Table 11.1 Types of Modules

Module Type	Encapsulated Information	Architecture Layer
Requirements encapsulation	System external interfaces (stimulus–response)	Functionality
Design decision-hiding	Design decisions (e.g., data structures, algorithms)	Common service
Hardware interface-hiding	Hardware interfaces	Common service

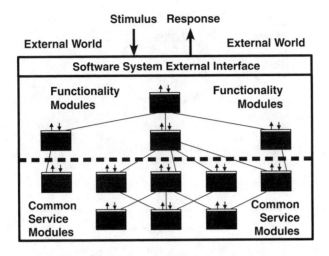

Figure 11.4   Canonical design architecture.

hiding modules. Requirements encapsulation modules exist to implement the requirements and provide the required functionality of the software; hence, they are called "functionality" modules. The design and hardware-hiding modules exist to provide common services for the requirements encapsulation modules; hence, they are called "common services" modules. These three module types are canonical to all OO applications developed using Freedom.

The dependencies among the three module types lead to a natural layering, or stratification, of modules based on their encapsulated information, as illustrated in Figure 11.4. The requirements encapsulating functionality modules make use of the design and hardware-hiding common services modules, but not vice versa. Also, the common services modules make use of each other. Thus, functionality modules occupy an upper stratum logically under the external interface (requirements) and users that they serve, whereas the common service modules occupy a lower stratum beneath the functionality modules that they serve. This stratification into two layers applies to all OO applications developed using Freedom, and so is called the "canonical design architecture."

Two basic relationships exist within and between the two strata of the canonical design architecture. As seen previously, the "activates" (NSR) relationship binds the functionality modules into a hierarchy (or a weak network if repetitive stimulus sets are present). The stimulus "activates" relationship exists only within the upper, or functionality module, layer. Because functionality modules use the common service modules, a "uses" relationship exists between the two strata. Because common services also use each other, the "uses" relationship also exists within the lower, or

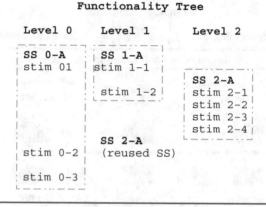

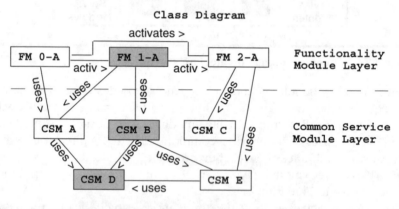

Figure 11.5   Design architecture for generic functionality tree.

common services, layer and gives the lower layer a strong network structure.

This layering and the relationships among the modules in each layer are illustrated in Figure 11.5. The figure expands Figure 11.3 to include a hypothetical set of common service modules (CSM) in the class diagram. Because these are OO modules, other OO relationships such as composition, inheritance, and polymorphism exist within both layers. These relationships constitute different views of the design architecture that are not depicted in Figure 11.5.

Each requirement typically has a vertical thread of dependencies through both layers of the canonical architecture. For example, assume a GUI button implements stimulus stim 1 – 1 of stimulus set SS 1 – A in Figure 11.5. For simplicity, assume the response behavior of stim 1 – 1 is the null response (do nothing). According to the design rule, the button object and its associated response behavior are implemented by, and encapsulated within, FM 1 – A in the functionality module layer. That is,

Table 11.2   Module Layering for Graphics Subsystem

Module Type	Encapsulated Information	Architecture Layer
Reqmts. encap.: graphical user interface (GUI)	Graphical components and their external responses	Functionality (upper)
Design-hiding: graphics package	Graphics data structures and algorithms	Common service (middle)
Hardware-hiding: graphics driver	Graphics hardware interfaces	Common service (lower)

the code of FM 1 – A instantiates a button object and handles the "button press" event of stim 1 – 1. Where is the code for a button defined? The button class is a common service module, such as CSM B in Figure 11.5. The requirements encapsulation module FM 1 – A "uses" the button module CSM B when creating the button instance for stim 1 – 1. The button module CSM B, in turn, "uses" a graphical device driver, or hardware-hiding module, when drawing the button on the screen. This graphical hardware-hiding module is the common service module CSM D in the figure. Both the button and the driver modules reside in the common service layer of the canonical architecture.

This layered structure for a general GUI stimulus implementation (not just buttons) is summarized in tabular form in Table 11.2.

Common service modules, especially design decision-hiding modules, are the mainstay of traditional OO. It is ironic that traditional OO does not recognize functionality modules because the functionality module layer is the most important stratum of the canonical design architecture. Functionality modules not only implement and encapsulate the requirements that are the reason for the program's existence, but also provide the rationale for the existence of the common service modules. In effect, functionality modules are the conceptual center of the design, supported from below by the common service modules and accessed from above by the users to whom they provide required functionality. The central role of the functionality modules is evident from their central location in Figure 11.4. As explained in Chapter 13, functionality modules are also of central importance to the external interface prototype.

11.4 Example Problem Functionality Module Architecture

The prioritized functionality tree for the Furmasco inventory system, developed in Listing 9.2 and repeated at the top of Figure 11.6, is used

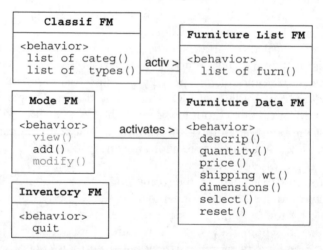

Figure 11.6 Inventory system Release 1 functionality module design.

by the development team as the basis for designing the external interface prototype.

*   *   *

Team Lead (of shipping department): The purpose of this meeting is to start the design of the interface prototype. We would like to give all the users in shipping a sneak preview of the user interface for the new inventory system, and gather any comments and suggestions for improvement they may have, prior to building the guts of the system.

IT Members: Agree. Yup! Let's do it!

Shipping Member 2: I read UML diagrams were the new way to do design.

Shipping Member 3: I heard CRC cards are more agile, or faster, or something. And all we need are some simple 3 × 5 note cards. Maybe we should do that.

IT Member 1: Those are both design techniques used by different methodologies. The Freedom methodology we are trying out here suggests UML for formal documentation, presentations to management, and the like. But for internal use by the team, it has a notation called an object model table, or OMT, which is faster and easier to create than UML and less cumbersome than CRC cards.

IT Member 2: That's right, but when developing an interface prototype, none of those design notations—not even the OMT—is needed. We just use the functionality tree as the design!

Shipping: I thought the functionality tree was part of the requirements, not design.

IT 1: The functionality tree does define the stimuli for the requirements, but it also defines the external interface architecture.

IT2: And the external interface architecture does double duty by serving as the top half of the design architecture, which is the part of the design applicable to an interface prototype.

Shipping: How does Freedom justify using requirements as design?

IT: By the requirements encapsulation design rule: create one functionality module for each unique stimulus set of the functionality tree. The purpose of the rule is to ensure that one requirement gets encapsulated in one code module for ease of change, but a side effect is that the requirements architecture and functionality module design architecture are identical.

Shipping: We have five stimulus sets in our functionality tree. So you are saying we only need five modules in the prototype?

IT: Almost. Remember, Furniture Data SS is repeated. Because only four stimulus sets are unique, the prototype will need only four functionality modules. But design for the prototype will basically look just like the functionality tree.

Team Lead: So the design is done. Well, that was quick! I reserved the conference room for all morning.

IT 1: Order some breakfast burritos and we can use the extra time for a Design Completion party. Ha ha!

Team Lead: Fine—you pay!

IT 1: Well . . .

Shipping 2: Darn! I was kind of hoping to draw some UML diagrams.

Team Lead: Hmm, because there will only be four boxes in total, go ahead. It will be good practice, and they will look nice for management. Let them know we are making progress.

IT 2: While he's doing that, us IT guys will take a copy of the functionality tree and start coding the functionality modules for the prototype.

IT 1: Start? By the time he's done with that UML drawing, we'll probably be *finished* with the prototype!

Team Lead: Down boys! Don't attack the nice shipping man.

IT 1: OK, we're outta here. Last one finished pays for lunch!

Shipping: You're on!

IT 2: Psst . . . what did you say that for?

*   *   *

The diagram produced by the shipping team members appears at the bottom of Figure 11.6.

Chapter 12

Requirements Encapsulation

12.1 Chapter Overview

This chapter discusses the implementation, or white box, concepts and techniques that are prerequisites of the construction of the interface mockup. These concepts and techniques build on the design concepts of Chapter 11, and serve the requirements process at the location highlighted in Figure 11.1. These white box concepts and techniques described in this chapter center on requirements encapsulating functionality modules. The chapter first illustrates the internal structure of a functionality module at a conceptual level, and contrasts it with the structure of a common service module. Next, the internal details of a functionality module are presented in the form of a generic coding template. Using the template, the chapter shows how the requirements notations of the functionality tree and behavior tables map directly to the parts of the coding template, thereby enabling a requirements-conforming executable interface mockup code to be created with minimal design effort.

This chapter is not a comprehensive exposition of the Freedom white box implementation process, which is outside the scope of this book. This chapter is concerned only with those aspects of implementation relevant to creation of an external interface prototype suitable for user verification of the requirements.

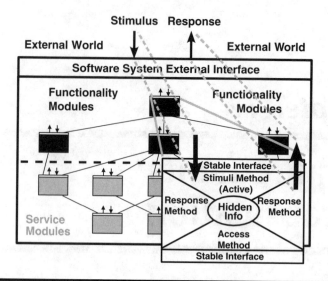

Figure 12.1   Functionality module architecture

12.2 Functionality Modules

The internal architecture of a functionality module consists of four major parts: (1) methods that implement stimuli, (2) methods that implement responses, (3) methods that provide external access to the module from other modules, and (4) the hidden information. Each functionality module in the upper stratum of the canonical design architecture has these four parts, as illustrated in Figure 12.1.

The methods that create stimuli project the stimuli to the external world consistent with the protocol specification. These methods also listen for stimulus input and perform any related event dispatching. In performing these functions, the stimulus methods rely on common service modules for lower-level details such as creation of graphical human interface components, listening for data or command signals, and event or interrupt handling.

Response behavior methods are invoked by the stimulus methods on receipt of stimuli. The response implementation methods directly encapsulate the external behavior specified in the behavior tables. Any internal components of the total behavior are performed by calling common service modules.

The hidden information is identical to the stimuli and responses implemented by, and encapsulated within, the stimulus methods and response methods just described.

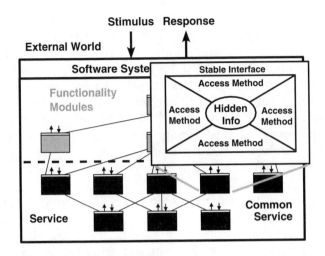

Figure 12.2 Common service module architecture

Access methods allow other modules of the application to access information encapsulated within the module, such as data obtained via data stimuli. Access methods are conceptually equivalent to the methods of a common service module, and should have a stable interface just as the methods of a common service module do.

12.3 Common Service Modules

The internal architecture of a common service module consists of three major parts: (1) some hidden information, (2) methods that provide external access to the hidden information from other modules, and (3) a stable interface to the access programs. Each common service module in the lower stratum of the canonical design architecture has these three parts, as illustrated in Figure 12.2.

The hidden information of a common service module includes software interfaces to hardware and design decisions such as algorithms and data structures. This is no different than in current OO practice. In addition, in Freedom, some common service modules encapsulate the internal part of required response behaviors, for example, business rules.

The access methods allow other modules of the application to indirectly access the hidden information of the module via the stable interface, rather than accessing the information directly. If the interface to the methods is stable, no other modules will need to change when the implementation of the hidden information changes, as described in Chapter 2. Again, this is identical to current OO practice.

In current OO design, common service modules comprise the entire application. However, in the canonical design architecture of Freedom, common service modules exist primarily to provide services needed by the upper strata functionality modules, and secondarily to provide services to each other. Such services include math packages, container or storage objects, and searching and sorting packages, to name a few. As described above, common services also provide business rules and logic that are not externally visible, that is, are not part of the requirements and thus encapsulated within functionality modules. Support of the functionality modules directly or indirectly provides the rationale for existence of all common service modules.

When a modern OO language such as Java is used to implement the application, an interesting thing happens in the common service layer: most if not all of the hardware-hiding modules disappear! This is because the "virtual machine" of a Java-like language effectively information-hides the entire machine. In effect, all common hardware-hiding modules are subsumed into the virtual machine and cease to be part of the application itself. Applications implemented with such languages can be moved from one machine to another in executable binary form with no change. Simplification of the common service layer by elimination of most hardware-hiding modules is a major advantage of virtual machine-based environments such as Java.

In conclusion, Freedom does not alter current OO, but rather extends OO to include requirements encapsulation. In so doing, it moves the external interface to the forefront, functionality modules to the center in support of the external interface, and common service modules to the bottom where they look to the functionality modules above for their purpose in life.

12.4 Functionality Module Structure

As with any other OO module, a functionality module consists of methods and modulewide field data. However, the nature of the module, its methods, and field data are tailored to encapsulation of requirements (stimulus–response pairs), as follows.

1. The module is named after the stimulus set that it implements.
2. Hidden information is the implementation details of the stimulus–response pairs of the stimulus set.
3. One or more stimulus methods implement the external interface protocols that project the stimuli to the user or environment.
4. One or more stimulus methods are responsible for the data and algorithms that implement stimulus detection, identification, and event dispatching.

5. One response method per stimulus implements the data and algorithms of the external component of the response behavior for that stimulus.
6. One or more access methods allow other modules access to needed data of the module consistent with conventional data-hiding practice.

A Java template for a functionality module is shown in Listings 12.1 and 12.2. Listing 12.1 depicts the code structure for the stimulus methods, and Listing 12.2 does so for the response methods. The template has been divided between two listings for ease of printing in this book, and contains line numbers for convenience of explanation. In actual usage, the template is the concatenation of the code in the two listings with the line number removed.

The following subsections discuss the parts of a functionality module with respect to the coding template.

12.4.1 Functionality Module Declaration

A functionality module is implemented as an OO class. It is named after the stimulus set that it implements in order to simplify traceability between stimulus sets (requirements) and their implementing code. See Listing 12.1, line 3.

Functionality modules that implement repetitive and reusable stimulus sets may take one of several forms depending on their nature.

1. They may be declared as a subclass of another functionality module if the requirements are a specialization of another stimulus set; for example, additional stimulus–response pairs are being added to the parent stimulus set (see Listing 12.1, line 3).
2. They may be an object instantiated from the functionality module (class) of the parent stimulus set if aspects of the stimuli, behavior, or their implementation protocol are parametrically configurable.
3. They may be the same functionality object that implements the parent stimulus set if everything about the repetitive stimulus sets is identical to the parent stimulus set.

12.4.2 Functionality Module Stimulus Methods

The protocol of the stimuli, such as human interface look and feel and programmatic input stream formats, are implemented by the constructor and associated special-purpose stimulus methods, such as createStimuli()

Listing 12.1   Functionality Module Template, Stimulus Code

```
01 // ***********************************************************
02 //                      functionality module for stimulus set <SS name>
03 class <SS_name> extends <superclass> {

04 //                      field data declarations for stimuli
05   private <reference_type> stimulus_1;
06   private <reference_type> stimulus_2;

07 //                      field data declarations for response behavior
08   private <reference_type> behavior_variable;

09 // ***********************************************************
10 //                      Stimulus Methods
11 //
12 //                      activation method (constructor)
13   public <SS_name>() {
14 //                      create stimuli
15     createStimuli();
16 //                      perform initialization response
17     initResponse();
18   }                     // end of activation method

19 // =========================================================
20 //                      method for creating stimuli of the stimulus set
21   private void createStimuli() {
22 //                      create stimuli objects
23     stimulus_1 = new <reference_type>();
24     stimulus_2 = new <reference_type>();
25 //                      For human UIs, layout the stimuli look and feel
26     <human UI layout code>
27 //                      enable stimuli
28     <stimulus activation code>
29   }                     // end of method for creating stimuli

30 // =========================================================
31 //                      method for detecting stimulus events
32   public void handleEvents() {
33     if (<event is from stimulus_1>) {
34       stimulus1Response();
35     }
36     else if (<event is from stimulus_2>) {
37       stimulus2Response();
38     }
39   }                     // end of method for detecting stimulus events

40 // ***********************************************************
                          [response code follows]
```

in Listing 12.1, lines 19 to 29. The constructor also calls the response method that performs the initialization response, if any, specified by the behavior table. See Listing 12.1, lines 9 to 18.

Listing 12.2   Functionality Module Template, Response Code

```
                        [stimulus code precedes]

41 // ************************************************************
42 //                    Response Methods
43 //
44 //                 method that performs initialization response
45   private void initResponse() {
46 //                    <behavior spec for init stimulus>
47     <implementing code for external behavior>
48 //                 invoke common services for internal behavior
49     commonServiceMethod();    // zero or more calls
50   }                    // end of init response method

51 // ============================================================
52 //                 method that performs response for stimulus_1
53   private void stimulus1Response() {
54 //                    <behavior spec for stimulus_1 response>
55     <implementing code for external behavior>
56 //                 invoke common services for internal behavior
57     commonServiceMethod();    // zero or more calls
58   }                    // end of stimulus_1 response method

59 // ============================================================
60 //                 method that performs response for stimulus_2
61   private void stimulus2Response() {
62 //                    <behavior spec for stimulus_2 response>
63     <implementing code for external behavior>
64 //                 invoke common services for internal behavior
65     commonServiceMethod();    // zero or more calls
66   }                    // end of stimulus_2 response method

67 // ************************************************************
68 //                    Access Methods
69 //
70 //                 method to <get field variable>
71   public <reference-type> get<variable>() {
72     <implementing code>
73   }                    // end of <get field variable> method

74 // ============================================================
75 //
76 //                 method to <set field variable>
77   public void set<variable>(<arguments>) {
78     <implementing code>
79   }                    // end of <set field variable> method

80 // ************************************************************

81 }                    // end of module for stimulus set <SS name>
```

The constructor also activates stimulus event detection. In addition, an event handler method detects and identifies stimulus events and dispatches control to the appropriate response method. See Listing 12.1, lines 17 and

30 to 39. Event detection will usually employ separate threads of control so that stimuli can be continually monitored and independently handled on different interface channels. These threads of control are denoted in Figure 12.1 by the stimulus method being labeled as "Active." Note that in languages such as Java, the system automatically provides this thread of control for graphical interfaces, but the programmer must explicitly create them using common service modules for "always on" network interfaces.

12.4.3 Functionality Module Response Methods

One method per stimulus is created to encapsulate the external (normal, NSR, and error) response specified in the behavior table for each stimulus. A separate response method is created to encapsulate any initialization stimulus. See Listing 12.2, lines 41 to 66. These same response methods call common service methods to perform internal components of the total response behavior. See Listing 12.2, lines 49, 57, and 65. The appropriate response method is called by the stimulus event handler method when a stimulus is received.

As an aid to implementation of the required response behavior, the "Body" statements of the structured English or PDL from the behavior table are copied verbatim into the response methods as comments. The code that implements each clause of the response behavior is placed immediately below its authorizing comment from the behavior table, providing traceability from requirements to implementation at an individual line of code level of detail. See Listing 12.2, lines 46 and 47, 54 and 55, and 62 and 63. Similarly, code that implements internal behavior (Constraints and Guidance) appears below the respective behavior table comments in the form of method calls to common services modules that encapsulate internal behavior such as "business rules." See Listing 12.2, lines 48 and 49, 56 and 57, and 64 and 65.

The above guideline regarding segregation of internal behavior code into common service modules should be adhered to unless the quality requirements indicate another mapping of the internal behavior to code modules results in improved quality. In all cases, however, external behavior code should be encapsulated within response methods of the functionality module.

12.4.4 Functionality Module Access Methods

Access methods are created as needed to permit other modules access to needed data within the functionality module, such as data obtained via data stimuli. These access methods are identical in every way to current OO practice. See Listing 12.2, lines 67 to 80.

12.4.5 Functionality Module Hidden Information

Functionality module hidden information includes stimulus methods that implement stimuli protocol and detection, response methods that implement required behavior, and all field data. To say that these entities are "hidden" means that they are declared "private" or are otherwise visibility-restricted to preclude direct access by other modules. See Listing 12.1, lines 5 to 8 and 21, and Listing 12.2, lines 45, 53, and 61. Also note in Figure 12.1 the lack of an external interface on the response methods, denoting their interfaces are visibility-restricted.

In some cases, the rules of the implementation language preclude certain of these methods from being visibility-restricted. For example, the constructor (Listing 12.1, line 13) and event handler (Listing 12.1, line 32) must be public by the inheritance rules of Java. In such cases, the rules of the language must be followed, but care should be taken to minimize access to these methods by other modules. In particular, common service modules should rarely, if ever, access the stimulus and response methods of functionality modules.

12.4.6 Functionality Module External Interface

The external interface to a functionality module consists of two parts: a stable programmatic interface and the software system external interface implemented by the encapsulated stimuli and response methods.

The programmatic interface to a functionality module consists of the interface to the stimulus method that creates the functionality object, for example, the constructor, as well as the interfaces to any access methods. The programmatic interface is used by other modules to activate the functionality module or to obtain needed data from the module. Because it is accessed by other modules, this programmatic interface should be stable, that is, unlikely to change should the requirements encapsulated by the functionality module change, as illustrated in Figure 12.1 by the regions labeled "Stable Interface."

The software system external interface of a functionality module is the portion of the program interface projected to the environment by the module. This may consist of graphical interfaces to humans, or protocol recognition and parsing code for programmatic interfaces to external systems or the environment. The software system external interface is represented in Figure 12.1 as two large arrows. The external interface is volatile, or likely to change during the life of the software, rather than stable, and so is encapsulated by the functionality module.

The interfaces to the response methods also need not be stable. Because response methods are visibility-restricted for internal use only, the interfaces to these methods are free to change when their encapsulated protocol or required behavior changes. This is indicated in Figure 12.1 by the lack of any "Stable Interface" region on the response methods.

12.5 Example Problem Functionality Module

After the meeting of the Furmasco development team at which the design of the inventory system mockup was discussed, the team members from IT begin work on the code for the mockup.

> IT 1: Do you think we should start with the top functionality module that implements Inventory SS, or with one of the lower-level ones?

> IT 2: If we start at the top, we have to write stub classes to test it, so let's start bottom up. It won't make much difference anyway because writing these prototypes goes fast in Java. We'll be done today, but probably not by lunch—that was a dumb bet.

> IT 1: Got carried away; didn't realize it was so late. Sorry. I'll pay.

> IT 2: Well, let's hustle and maybe you won't have to. Let's start with Furniture List SS.

They copy the functionality module template to the source code development directory and rename the file FurnitureList.java. The class name is declared to be FurnitureList.

> IT 2: Now let's create the stimulus methods. What are the names of the stimuli for Furniture List SS?

> IT 1: The functionality tree (Listing 9.2) only shows one. It's called "list of furniture." In the functionality screen (Listing 6.7), it looks like a List component.

> IT 2: OK, then let's create a List component named list_of_furniture to match the requirements as closely as possible.

After creating the list, they create two response methods named listOfFurnitureResponse() and initResponse() to encapsulate the behavior specified in the behavior table of Listing 10.9.

> IT 1: Now the fun part. We get to retype the behavior PDL into the two response methods as comments.

> IT 2: Well, you can retype it all if you want, but I'm going to use cut and paste to just copy them in. I'm trying to save you from paying for lunch, guy.

> IT 1: Good idea. Maybe some day someone will write a tool to generate functionality module code for the mockup prototype right from the behavior tables.

> IT 2: That would be nice. You'd win your bet with shipping for sure then! We really would have the mockup finished and running before they could draw a UML diagram.

> IT 1: Maybe the tool could draw the UML diagram from the behavior table, too.

> IT 2: You could probably generate UML right from the functionality tree. But why bother? Some people say that code is the best measure of progress.

> IT 1: With tools like that, I'd say a functionality tree and behavior tables are all the progress you need. The code would fall right out.

> IT 2: Just about.

The body statements of the behavior table are copied verbatim to the methods in the form of comments to guide creation of the response code, and help ensure the implementation precisely matches the requirements. The listOfFurnResponse() response method is called by the event handling method for the List component consistent with Java's event-handling conventions. A call to the initResponse() method is placed in the constructor. Listing 12.3 shows the completed functionality module.

> IT 2: One down, four to go.

> IT 1: Well, almost lunch time. Say we finish the mockup when we get back? We're not going to win the bet anyway. If we leave now, we'll beat the crowd.

Listing 12.3 Functionality Module for Furniture List SS

```
//  ******************************************************************
//                    functionality module for SS FurnitureList

package com.furmasco.inventory.gui;

import java.awt.Panel;
import java.awt.Label;
import java.awt.List;
import java.awt.BorderLayout;
import java.awt.event.ItemListener;
import java.awt.event.ItemEvent;

class FurnitureList extends Panel implements ItemListener {

//                    data declarations for stimuli
  private List list_of_furniture;

//                    data declarations for response behavior support
  private Label ss_label;
  private Inventory inventory_app;

//  ******************************************************************
//                    Stimulus Methods
//
//                    activation method (constructor)
  public FurnitureList () {
//                    save reference to main program
    inventory_app = Inventory.getInventory();

//                    create stimuli
    createStimuli();
//                    perform initialization response
    initResponse();
  }                   // end of activation method

//  ================================================================
//                    method for creating stimuli of the stimulus set
  private void createStimuli() {

//                    create stimuli objects
    ss_label = new Label ("List of Furniture",
                      Label.CENTER);

    list_of_furniture = new List();

//                    For human UIs, layout the stimuli look and feel
    layoutStimuli();
//                    enable list_of_furnitureories stimuli
    list_of_furniture.addItemListener (this);
  }                   // end of method for creating stimuli

//  ================================================================
```

Listing 12.3   Functionality Module for Furniture List SS (continued)

```
//                  method for laying out an UI stimulus set
   private void layoutStimuli() {

      this.setLayout (new BorderLayout());
      this.add (ss_label, BorderLayout.NORTH);
      this.add (list_of_furniture, BorderLayout.CENTER);
   }                // end of method for  out an UI stimulus set

// ================================================================
//                  method for detecting stimulus events
   public void itemStateChanged (ItemEvent ie) {
      Object stimulus = ie.getSource();
      if (stimulus ==  list_of_furniture) {
        listOfFurnitureResponse();
      }
   }                // end of method for detecting stimulus events

// ****************************************************************
//                  Response Methods
//
//                  method that performs initialization response
   private void initResponse() {
//                  IF selected_type is set
//                  THEN
//                     clear list_of_furniture stimuli
//                     display list_of_furnitureiture for selected_type
//                      as new list_of_furniture stimuli
//                  END IF
   }                // end of init response method

// ================================================================
//                  method that performs response for list_of_furniture
   private void listOfFurnitureResponse() {
//                  highlight selected_furn_item
//   (intrinsic to List component)
//                  display descrip, quantity, price, shipping wt,
//                  dimensions for selected_furn_item in FurnData SS
//   <implementing code for external behavior>
   }                // end of list_of_furniture response method

}                   // end of module for stimulus set FurnitureList
// ****************************************************************
```

IT 2: The shipping guys will probably want to finish their UML diagram first.

IT 1: Tough.

Chapter 13

Interface Prototyping

13.1 Chapter Overview

The Freedom requirements process, shown for reference in Figure 13.1, specifies that an interface mockup be created to obtain user verification of the requirements. This chapter explains why a mockup is used and not some other form of prototype. The different types of prototypes are reviewed and their utility is compared. The result of the comparison is a clear recommendation for use of an interface mockup, along with an understanding of why.

13.2 Purpose of Prototypes

In many manufacturing disciplines, a prototype is built for proof-of-concept or evaluation purposes. A prototype helps reduce risk by eliminating potentially costly mistakes before the product goes into production. In software, the purpose of a prototype is often the same, that is, risk reduction. In addition, a software prototype can be used for clarification of requirements, obtaining user commitment, training, demonstration, and evaluation of proposed solutions.[1]

13.2.1 Clarify Requirements

Clarifying requirements is one of the primary means of reducing software risk. Even though a knowledgeable user representative is involved in the requirements specification process, risk can be further reduced by obtaining

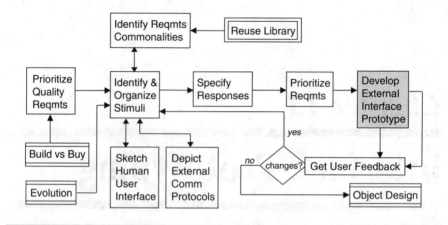

Figure 13.1   Interface prototyping in the requirements process.

requirements feedback from as large a number of customer personnel as possible. A prototype gives customers and developers alike the opportunity to identify missing or incorrect functionality while exercising the prototype. Even if very little actual functionality in the prototype works, a prototype is one of the better vehicles for verifying the correctness and completeness of requirements.

13.2.2 Obtain User Commitment

When customer personnel become familiar with a prototype, they often develop a sense of loyalty to the new software. This can often be an effective way of obtaining user commitment to the software project. The prototype also sets a level of expectation with the users as to what to expect in the final product. Risk can be associated with this expectation if the final product differs significantly from the prototype without the user being made aware of the changes, such as by release of another prototype.

Another risk associated with a prototype, particularly one with a release-quality user interface, is that some users may conclude the software is nearly finished when in fact the project is just beginning. Such risk can be mitigated by taking care to inform the customer personnel as to the true nature of the prototype.

13.2.3 Training

A prototype can be an effective vehicle for training customer personnel in the use of new software prior to availability of the final product. Of course, complete training may not be possible inasmuch as the prototype is likely to have significant missing functionality. However, implementing critical or high-usage functionality first allows users of the prototype to become familiar with key capabilities, allowing a quicker and smoother transition to the final product when it is released.

13.2.4 Demonstration

A prototype can allow the customer to demonstrate future capabilities to their external suppliers and associates in a concrete way. Using a prototype for demonstration can provide public relations benefits in addition to all the previously mentioned benefits and risks associated with clarification of requirements, commitment, and training.

13.2.5 Evaluate Solutions

Although the previously stated benefits of a prototype relate to the customer, a prototype can also be targeted to developer issues. For example, a prototype can help assess the merits of design alternatives by gathering information such as performance, memory demand, and usability factors. This information can be used as input to quality requirement analysis to select among design alternatives based on the customer's priorities for quality.

13.3 Types of Prototypes

A prototype applicable to requirements verification is one that fully or partially implements the functionality modules. Such an "interface" proto-type can be characterized by the fidelity of the implemented functionality modules, including

- Completeness of the stimuli methods;
- Completeness of required behavior, including
  - Normal responses,
  - New stimulus responses (NSR),
  - Error responses, and
  - Performance, accuracy, precision (PAP) requirements.

The combinations inherent in these factors are reflected in the Interface Prototype Classification List, shown in Table 13.1. This table identifies nine categories of interface prototypes.

Table 13.1   Interface Prototype Classification List

Stimuli Methods	Normal Response	New Stim Response	Error + PAP Response	Name of Prototype
Part	Part	Part	Part	Partial functional simulation
Part	Full	Part	Part	Vertical functional simulation
Part	Full	Part	Full	Robust vertical functional simulation
Part	Part	Full	Part	External interface simulation
Part	Full	Full	Part	Full functional simulation
Part	Full	Full	Full	Robust functional simulation
Full	Part	Full	Part	External interface mockup
Full	Full	Full	Part	Full functional mockup
Full	Full	Full	Full	Release

Full = fully implemented.
Part = partially implemented or not implemented.

1. Partial Functional Simulation
2. Vertical Functional Simulation
3. Robust Vertical Functional Simulation
4. External Interface Simulation
5. Full Functional Simulation
6. Robust Functional Simulation
7. External Interface Mockup
8. Full Functional Mockup
9. Release

Each of the nine interface prototype variants is discussed individually below.

13.3.1 Partial Functional Simulation

■ *Stimuli Methods:* partially implemented (actual L&F (look and feel) not implemented)

- *Normal Response:* partially implemented
- *New Stimulus Response:* partially implemented
- *Error and PAP Response:* partially or not implemented

A partial functional simulation is used to evaluate the quality of alternative design and implementation solutions, which will usually be at the common service level. This is accomplished by implementing one or more stimulus sets that utilize the solutions of interest. If any of the implemented stimulus sets are lower-level, the new stimulus responses necessary to activate them are also implemented. The normal, error, and PAP required behaviors that utilize the alternative design solutions are, of course, also implemented.

In a simulation (as opposed to a mockup), functionality module stimulus methods do not paint the final look and feel. They may, in fact, use totally different interface technology than is planned for the release, for example, a textual interface instead of a graphical one. However, external system and environment interfaces should conform to the actual protocols for proper evaluation. Thus, "interface simulation" means the look and feel is simulated rather than being in proper or final form.

13.3.2 Vertical Functional Simulation

- *Stimuli Methods:* partially implemented (L&F not implemented)
- *Normal Response:* fully implemented subset
- *New Stimulus Response:* partially implemented
- *Error and PAP Response:* partially or not implemented

A vertical functional simulation is used to fully evaluate a subset of the required functionality, usually some key aspect of the requirements around which other parts of the application revolve. This usually involves implementing, at a minimum, the functionality modules that encapsulate the requirements of interest, including all of their normal and NSR responses plus the stimuli methods that activate the external interface. The latter may or may not conform to the desired final look and feel for human interfaces, but should conform to the actual protocols for external system and environment interfaces. Most important, the normal response behavior must be fully implemented so the requirements of interest can be verified as correct by actual usage with suitable test data or realistic field tasks. Associated PAP requirements must also be fully implemented, but error responses need not be (see Section 13.3.3 below).

13.3.3 Robust Vertical Functional Simulation

- *Stimuli Methods:* partially implemented (L&F not implemented)
- *Normal Response:* fully implemented subset
- *New Stimulus Response:* partially implemented
- *Error and PAP Response:* fully implemented subset

A robust vertical functional simulation is a vertical functional simulation in which the error responses for the functionality being evaluated are also fully implemented.

13.3.4 External Interface Simulation

- *Stimuli Methods:* partially implemented (L&F not implemented)
- *Normal Response:* partially or not implemented
- *New Stimulus Response:* fully implemented
- *Error and PAP Response:* partially or not implemented

An external interface simulation is used to quickly obtain customer feedback on the functionality available via the external interface. All functionality module stimuli activation methods are implemented along with all NSR responses, but the external interface does not conform to the final look and feel or protocol. It may, in fact, use totally different interface technology than is planned for the release, for example, a textual interface instead of a graphical one. Normal and error responses are partially implemented at best, and may be totally absent.

13.3.5 Full Functional Simulation

- *Stimuli Methods:* partially implemented (L&F not implemented)
- *Normal Response:* fully implemented
- *New Stimulus Response:* fully implemented
- *Error and PAP Response:* partially or not implemented

A full functional simulation is used to evaluate all required functionality except error responses. This involves implementing all functionality modules, including all normal and NSR responses plus the stimuli methods that activate the external interface. The latter may or may not conform to the desired final look and feel for human interfaces, but should conform to the actual protocols for external system and environment interfaces. Most important, all normal responses must be fully implemented so the required functionality can be verified as correct by actual usage with suitable test data or field tasks. Thus, all common service modules needed to support the normal responses must also be implemented. Associated PAP requirements must also be fully implemented, but error responses need not be (see Section 13.3.6 below).

13.3.6 Robust Functional Simulation

- *Stimuli Methods:* partially implemented (L&F not implemented)
- *Normal Response:* fully implemented
- *New Stimulus Response:* fully implemented
- *Error and PAP Response:* fully implemented

A robust functional simulation is a full functional simulation in which all error responses are fully implemented. If the human interface of a robust functional simulation conforms to the final desired look and feel, then the prototype is a release (see Section 13.3.9 below).

13.3.7 External Interface Mockup

- *Stimuli Methods:* fully implemented
- *Normal Response:* partially or not implemented
- *New Stimulus Response:* fully implemented
- *Error and PAP Response:* partially or not implemented

An external interface mockup is used to obtain customer feedback on all aspects of the requirements except required behavior. It may also be used to obtain user commitment to the new software, to provide pre-release training, or serve demonstration needs. All stimuli methods are fully implemented and project all stimuli using the actual look and feel and protocols. All NSR responses are implemented. Normal and error responses may be totally absent, or simulated such as by hard-coding a typical response.

The term "interface mockup" means the prototype looks like the real thing externally, but is mostly a hollow shell internally.

13.3.8 Full Functional Mockup

- *Stimuli Methods:* fully implemented
- *Normal Response:* fully implemented

- *New Stimulus Response:* fully implemented
- *Error and PAP Response:* partially or not implemented

A full functional mockup serves the same purposes as an external interface mockup. All stimuli methods are fully implemented and project all stimuli using the actual look and feel and protocols. All normal and NSR responses, and all common service modules needed to support these responses, are fully implemented. Error responses may be partially or totally absent. If all error responses of a full functional mockup are also implemented, then the prototype is a release (see Section 13.3.9 below).

13.3.9 Release

- *Stimuli Methods:* fully implemented
- *Normal Response:* fully implemented
- *New Stimulus Response:* fully implemented
- *Error and PAP Response*: fully implemented

A release is a fully implemented software system. All requirements slated for the release are fully functional with all stimuli methods in final form; all normal, NSR, error, and PAP requirements met; and all supporting common service modules complete. Whether a release is considered a prototype is a matter of development process management. For example, some projects field a completed release to a select group of users to obtain feedback prior to mass distribution, sometimes called a "beta release" or "beta test." Other projects may simply ship the completed release to the customer. In the former case, the release can be considered a prototype as the goal is to obtain additional development feedback. In the latter case, it is not a prototype because any feedback received would enter the life-cycle process via the evolution process.

13.3.10 Which To Use?

With so many prototype variations to choose from, which one should be used? The answer is that it depends on which aspects of the requirements are being evaluated. However, one characteristic shared by most require-ments prototyping is the desire to evaluate the requirements quickly without implementing the bulk of the software system, that is, the common service modules. Three of the above prototype variants meet this criterion by virtue of not implementing required response behavior, and are there-fore most suitable for rapid requirements evaluation. These three, which are highlighted in Table 13.1, are:

Table 13.2 Interface Prototype Utility

Purpose	UI Mockup	UI Sim	PF Sim
Clarify requirements	Yes	Some	No
Obtain user commitment	Yes	Some	No
Training	Yes	No	No
Demonstration	Yes	Some	No
Evaluate solutions	No	No	Yes

- Partial Functional Simulation (1)
- External Interface Simulation (4)
- External Interface Mockup (7)

These three prototype variants are compared side by side in the Table 13.2 to highlight the degree to which each is able to accomplish the five purposes of a prototype enumerated earlier.

The table makes it clear that a partial function simulation is the option of choice for evaluation of solution alternatives. For all other purposes, the external interface mockup provides the best utility. In addition, an external interface mockup can also serve to evaluate solutions by implementing a subset of required behavior of interest. Because an external interface mockup can double as a partial function simulation, the external interface mockup is the prototype of choice in nearly all situations.

13.4 Example Problem Interface Mockup

On return from lunch, the IT members of the Furmasco inventory system development team resume work on the external interface mockup. Functionality modules for the Furniture Data, Classification, Mode, and Inventory stimulus sets are developed in the same manner as the Furniture List module was previously (see Chapter 12). Because an external interface mockup implements the actual look and feel, the stimuli methods are fully implemented.

*   *   *

IT 2: This createStimuli() method is getting pretty big. Most of it is code for arranging the components. Maybe we should put all this layout code in its own method.

Table 13.3   Stimulus Creation Method Trade-Off

Rank	Quality Attribute	Layout Code with Stimulus Creation	Layout Code in Own Method
1	Functionality	Unaffected (but cannot support multiple layouts)	Unaffected (but can support multiple layouts)
2	Reliability	Unaffected	Unaffected
3	Maintainability	Potentially harder	**Potentially easier**
4	Usability	Unaffected	Unaffected
5	Administerability	Unaffected	Unaffected
6	Execution speed	No significant difference	No significant difference
7	Storage demand	No significant difference	No significant difference

IT 1: Two smaller methods or one larger method to create the stimuli? Wouldn't two methods be unnecessary fragmentation? After all, it's all the same task: creating the stimuli. Maybe one method is better. Just isolate the layout code with "horizontal line" comments.

IT 2: Time for the quality requirements.

IT 1: Right!

They trade off the two alternatives using a table similar to that of Table 13.3. Most quality attributes are unaffected, but one is decisive.

IT 2: Functionality can be better supported by the layout code being in its own method, for example, support of more than one layout arrangement. Maybe the createStimulus() method calls one of several layout methods based on a command line parameter. So Functionality is better for the "own method" option.

IT 1: Clever idea. But none of the shipping guys said anything about a stimulus that would select a different layout. There is no requirement for that functionality.

IT 2: Not now, but if there were in the future, it would make maintainability easier because the code would already be structured to accommodate it.

IT 1: OK. So maintainability is potentially easier if multiple arrangements are ever needed. But I don't think it's fair to say functionality is an advantage when we have no requirement for multiple layouts. We can indicate it as a possible advantage, but functionality should count as "unaffected" in the actual comparison. Potential maintainability is the only real advantage.

IT 2: Agreed. Because everything else is a wash, maintainability is the determining factor. Placing the layout code meets our quality requirements better.

IT 1: Looks that way. So we move all the layout code to its own method. How about calling it layoutStimuli()?

IT 2: Sounds good.

*   *   *

Other differences of opinion regarding implementation alternatives are resolved in a similar manner using the project quality requirements as evaluation criteria. By the end of the day, they are done with the prototype. The finished code is shown in Listings 13.1 to 13.4. The next morning, the entire team meets to assess progress.

IT: Did you guys have fun drawing your UML diagram?

Shipping: The new UML diagrammer tool is kind of complicated to use, but once you get the hang of it, the diagrams aren't too hard to draw. Just takes time. Here it is.

They hand the IT members a copy of Figure 11.6.

IT: The UML diagram looks just like the functionality tree. Only difference is there are more lines and arrows, and boxes around the stimulus sets.

Shipping: Yeah, we noticed that. I think from now on we'll just stick with the functionality tree because it's faster, unless we have to present it to management. The UML boxes and arrows

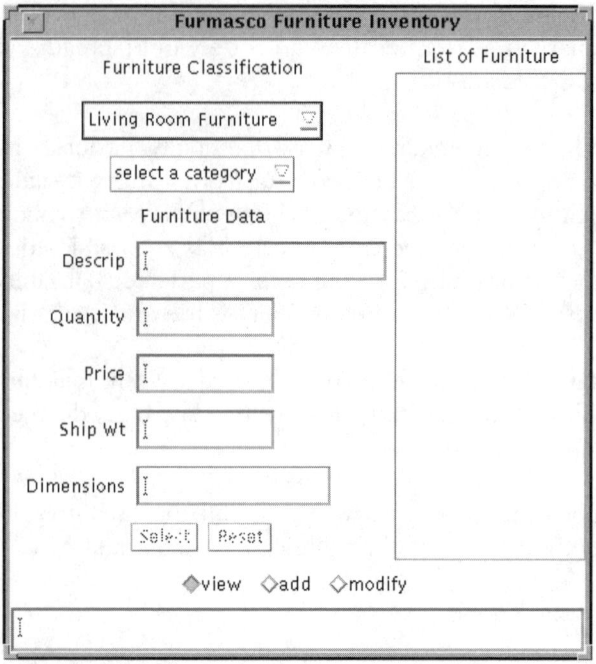

Figure 13.2   Inventory system external interface mockup screen shot.

are probably easier for managers to understand. How far along are you with the prototype?

IT: We're done. Want to come see?

Shipping: Already? That was quick! Yeah, show us.

They gather around the computer, and IT brings up the external interface mockup. The image on the screen looks like Figure 13.2.

Shipping: Hey, way to go! Let's put this on the server where the rest of shipping can get to it. There's a shipping staff meeting this afternoon. Why don't you IT guys attend and explain to everyone how to access it. We'll ask our management to have everyone in shipping try it out and see how they like it.

IT: OK. You realize this is only a mockup. Nothing actually works. We just need to know if any buttons or entry fields or anything else they need are missing. Also if everything that is there is really needed, is labeled correctly, and that sort of thing. But they shouldn't complain about it "not working" because it's not supposed to.

Shipping: We'll make that clear to management when we talk to them, and management and you guys can explain it to the troops. We should also point out that the initial release will be for data entry only, so only the "add" mode will work.

IT: Exactly. How long do you think everyone will need to try it and finish writing down their evaluations?

Shipping: The sooner the better so we can get going on the real thing. We'll suggest two days and see what they say.

IT: Sounds good. By the way, this mockup *is* the real thing. Unless the feedback says we totally missed the boat, we can just add to the mockup and grow it into the finished release. We hope we won't have to throw anything out except whatever needs to be revised based on the feedback.

Shipping: That's great! All right, we have a plan. You guys get it running on the server, and we'll talk to Shipping management. The meeting is at 2:00.

IT: See you then.

Listing 13.1 Functionality Module for Furniture Data SS

```
// ******************************************************************
//                    functionality module for SS FurnitureData

package com.furmasco.inventory.gui;

import java.awt.Panel;
import java.awt.Label;
import java.awt.Button;
import java.awt.TextField;
import java.awt.FlowLayout;
import java.awt.BorderLayout;
import java.awt.GridLayout;
import java.awt.event.ActionListener;
import java.awt.event.ActionEvent;

class FurnitureData extends Panel implements ActionListener {

//                    data declarations for stimuli
  private TextField descrip;
  private TextField quantity;
  private TextField price;
  private TextField ship_wt;
  private TextField dimens;
  private Button select;
  private Button reset;

//                    data declarations for response behavior support
  private Label ss_label;
  private Label descrip_label;
  private Label quantity_label;
  private Label price_label;
  private Label ship_wt_label;
  private Label dimens_label;
  private Inventory inventory_app;

// ******************************************************************
//                    Stimulus Methods
//
//                    activation method (constructor)
  public FurnitureData () {
//                    save reference to main program
    inventory_app = Inventory.getInventory();

//                    create stimuli
    createStimuli();
//                    perform initialization response
    initResponse();
  }                    // end of activation method

// ==================================================================
//                    method for creating stimuli of the stimulus set
  private void createStimuli() {
//                    create stimuli objects
```

Listing 13.1   Functionality Module for Furniture Data SS (continued)

```
    ss_label = new Label ("Furniture Data", Label.CENTER);
    descrip_label = new Label ("Descrip", Label.RIGHT);
    quantity_label = new Label ("Quantity", Label.RIGHT);
    price_label = new Label ("Price", Label.RIGHT);
    ship_wt_label = new Label ("Ship Wt", Label.RIGHT);
    dimens_label = new Label ("Dimensions", Label.RIGHT);


--------------------------------------------------------------------

    descrip = new TextField (20);
    quantity = new TextField (10);
    price = new TextField (10);
    ship_wt = new TextField (10);
    dimens = new TextField (15);
    select = new Button ("Select");
    reset = new Button ("Reset");

//                  For human UIs, layout the stimuli look and feel
    layoutStimuli();
//                  enable list_of_furniture stimuli
    descrip.addActionListener (this);
    quantity.addActionListener (this);
    price.addActionListener (this);
    ship_wt.addActionListener (this);
    dimens.addActionListener (this);
    select.addActionListener (this);
    reset.addActionListener (this);
  }                 // end of method for creating stimuli

// ==================================================================
//                  method for laying out an UI stimulus set
  private void layoutStimuli() {
    Panel label_panel = new Panel (new GridLayout(5,1));
    Panel field_panel = new Panel (new GridLayout(5,1));
    Panel labfld_panel = new Panel (new BorderLayout());
    Panel descrip_label_panel =
      new Panel (new FlowLayout(FlowLayout.LEFT));
    Panel quantity_label_panel =
      new Panel (new FlowLayout(FlowLayout.LEFT));
    Panel price_label_panel =
      new Panel (new FlowLayout(FlowLayout.LEFT));
    Panel ship_wt_label_panel =
      new Panel (new FlowLayout(FlowLayout.LEFT));
    Panel dimens_label_panel =
      new Panel (new FlowLayout(FlowLayout.LEFT));
    Panel button_panel = new Panel();

    descrip_label_panel.add (this.descrip);
    quantity_label_panel.add (this.quantity);
    price_label_panel.add (this.price);
    ship_wt_label_panel.add (this.ship_wt);
    dimens_label_panel.add (this.dimens);
    field_panel.add (descrip_label_panel);
    field_panel.add (quantity_label_panel);
```

Listing 13.1   Functionality Module for Furniture Data SS (continued)

```
      field_panel.add (price_label_panel);
      field_panel.add (ship_wt_label_panel);
      field_panel.add (dimens_label_panel);
      label_panel.add (this.descrip_label);
      label_panel.add (this.quantity_label);
      label_panel.add (this.price_label);
      label_panel.add (this.ship_wt_label);
      label_panel.add (this.dimens_label);
      labfld_panel.add (label_panel, BorderLayout.WEST);
      labfld_panel.add (field_panel, BorderLayout.CENTER);

      button_panel.add (select);
      button_panel.add (reset);

      this.setLayout (new BorderLayout());
      this.add (ss_label, BorderLayout.NORTH);
      this.add (labfld_panel, BorderLayout.CENTER);
      this.add (button_panel, BorderLayout.SOUTH);
   }                  // end of method for  out an UI stimulus set

// ================================================================
//                 method for detecting stimulus events
  public void actionPerformed (ActionEvent ae) {
    Object stimulus = ae.getSource();
    if (stimulus ==  descrip) {
      descripResponse();
    }
    else if (stimulus ==  quantity) {
      quantityResponse();
    }
    else if (stimulus ==  price) {
      priceResponse();
    }
    else if (stimulus ==  ship_wt) {
      shipWtResponse();
    }
    else if (stimulus ==  dimens) {
      dimensResponse();
    }
    else if (stimulus ==  select) {
      selectResponse();
    }
    else if (stimulus ==  reset) {
      resetResponse();
    }
  }                  // end of method for detecting stimulus events

// ****************************************************************
//                 Response Methods
//
//                 method that performs initialization response
  private void initResponse() {
```

Listing 13.1   Functionality Module for Furniture Data SS (continued)

```
//                  disable all stimuli of this SS for input
   disableStimuli();
//                  clear descrip, quantity, price, shipping wt,
//                    dimensions
   descrip.setText("");
   quantity.setText("");
   price.setText("");
   ship_wt.setText("");
   dimens.setText("");
 }                // end of init response method


// =================================================================
//                  method that performs response for descrip
  private void descripResponse() {
//                  echo description
//  (intrinsic to TextField component)
   }                  // end of descrip response method


// =================================================================
//                  method that performs response for quantity
  private void quantityResponse() {
//                  echo quantity
//  (intrinsic to TextField component)
//                  clear message area
//                  IF quantity not integral
//                  THEN
//                    display error message in message area
//                    display original quantity
//                  ELSE IF quantity is negative
//                  THEN
//                    display 'negative quantity deletes item' msg
//                      in message area
//                  END IF
   }                // end of quantity response method


// =================================================================
//                  method that performs response for price
  private void priceResponse() {
//                  echo price
//  (intrinsic to TextField component)
//                  clear message area
//                  IF price is not a number or
//                      price is negative or zero
//                  THEN
//                    display error message in message area
//                    display original price
//                  END IF
   }                // end of add response method


// =================================================================
//                  method that performs response for ship_wt
  private void shipWtResponse() {
```

Listing 13.1   Functionality Module for Furniture Data SS (continued)

```
//                    echo shipping wt
//   (intrinsic to TextField component)
//                    clear message area
//                    IF shipping wt is not a number or
//                       shipping wt is negative
//                    THEN
//                      display error message in message area
//                      display original shipping wt
//                    END IF
    }                 // end of add response method


//  =================================================================
//                    method that performs response for dimens
  private void dimensResponse() {
//                    echo dimensions
//   (intrinsic to TextField component)
//                    clear message area
//                    IF dimensions not comma separated 3 values or
//                       values are not all numbers or
//                       values are not all positive
//                    THEN
//                      display error message in message area
//                      display original dimensions
//                    END IF
    }                 // end of add response method


//  =================================================================
//                    method that performs response for select
  private void selectResponse() {
//                    clear message area
//                    IF any data field is blank
//                      display error message in message area
//                    ELSE IF quantity is negative
//                      delete descrip item from inventory
//                      remove descrip item from list_of_furniture
//                       in Furniture List SS
//                      display 'item deleted' message in message area
//                    ELSE
//                      update descrip item in inventory with
//                       quantity, price, shipping wt, dimensions
//                      display 'item saved' message in message area
//                    END IF
    }                 // end of add response method


//  =================================================================
//                    method that performs response for reset
  private void resetResponse() {
//                    IF selected_furn_item is set
//                       set descrip, quantity, price, ship wt, dimens
//                        in Furniture Data SS from selected_furn_item
//                    ELSE
//                      clear descrip, quantity, price, shipping wt,
```

Listing 13.1   Functionality Module for Furniture Data SS (continued)

```
//                    dimensions in Furniture Data SSS
//                 END IF
   }              // end of add response method

// *******************************************************************
//                 Access Methods
//
//                 method for disabling all stimuli of SS
  public void disableStimuli() {
    descrip.setEnabled (false);
    quantity.setEnabled (false);
    price.setEnabled (false);
    ship_wt.setEnabled (false);
    dimens.setEnabled (false);
    select.setEnabled (false);
    reset.setEnabled (false);
  }              // end of method for disabling all stimuli

// ==================================================================
//                 method for enabling all stimuli of SS
  public void enableStimuli() {
    descrip.setEnabled (true);
    quantity.setEnabled (true);
    price.setEnabled (true);
    ship_wt.setEnabled (true);
    dimens.setEnabled (true);
    select.setEnabled (true);
    reset.setEnabled (true);
  }              // end of method for enabling all stimuli

// ==================================================================
//                 method for enabling stimuli for modify
  public void enableStimuliForModify() {
    descrip.setEnabled (false);
    quantity.setEnabled (true);
    price.setEnabled (true);
    ship_wt.setEnabled (false);
    dimens.setEnabled (false);
    select.setEnabled (true);
    reset.setEnabled (true);
  }              // end of method for enabling stimuli for modify

}              // end of module for stimulus set FurnitureData
// *******************************************************************
```

Listing 13.2 Functionality Module for Classification SS

```
// ***************************************************************
//                 functionality module for SS Classification

package com.furmasco.inventory.gui;

import java.awt.Panel;
import java.awt.Label;
import java.awt.Choice;
import java.awt.GridLayout;
import java.awt.event.ItemListener;
import java.awt.event.ItemEvent;

class Classification extends Panel implements ItemListener {

//                 data declarations for stimuli
  private Choice list_of_categ;
  private Choice list_of_types;

//                 data declarations for response behavior support
  private Label ss_label;
  private String[] living_rm_types = {
    "Sofa",
    "Sofa bed",
    "Chair",
    "Table",
    "Shelves",
    "Lamp"
    };

  private String[] dining_rm_types = {
    "Table",
    "Chair",
    "Hutch"
    };

  private String[] bedrm_types = {
    "Bed",
    "Dresser",
    "Mirror",
    "Chest",
    "Table",
    "Lamp"
    };

  private String[] office_types = {
    "Desk",
    "Table",
    "Chair",
    "Shelves",
    "Lamp"
    };

  private Inventory inventory_app;
```

Listing 13.2 Functionality Module for Classification SS (continued)

```
// *********************************************************************
//                    Stimulus Methods
//
//                    activation method (constructor)
  public Classification () {
//                    save reference to main program
    inventory_app = Inventory.getInventory();

//                    create stimuli
    createStimuli();
//                    perform initialization response
    initResponse();
  }                   // end of activation method

// ===================================================================
//                    method for creating stimuli of the stimulus set
  private void createStimuli() {

//                    create stimuli objects
    ss_label = new Label ("Furniture Classification",
                          Label.CENTER);

    list_of_categ = new Choice();
    list_of_categ.add ("Living Room Furniture");
    list_of_categ.add ("Dining Room Furniture");
    list_of_categ.add ("Bedroom Furniture");
    list_of_categ.add ("Office Furniture");

    list_of_types = new Choice();
    list_of_types.add ("select a category");

//                    For human UIs, layout the stimuli look and feel
    layoutStimuli();
  }                   // end of method for creating stimuli

// ===================================================================
//                    method for laying out an UI stimulus set
  private void layoutStimuli() {
    Panel categ_panel = new Panel();
    Panel types_panel = new Panel();

    categ_panel.add (list_of_categ);
    types_panel.add (list_of_types);

    this.setLayout (new GridLayout (3,1));
    this.add (ss_label);
    this.add (categ_panel);
    this.add (types_panel);
  }                   // end of method for  out an UI stimulus set

// ===================================================================
//                    method for detecting stimulus events
  public void itemStateChanged (ItemEvent ie) {
```

Listing 13.2 Functionality Module for Classification SS (continued)

```
   Object stimulus = ie.getSource();
   if (stimulus ==  list_of_categ) {
     listOfCategResponse();
   }
   else if (stimulus ==  list_of_types) {
     listOfTypesResponse();
   }
 }                     // end of method for detecting stimulus events

// *****************************************************************
//                    Response Methods
//
//                    method that performs initialization response
 private void initResponse() {
//                    enable list_of_categories stimuli
   list_of_categ.addItemListener (this);
   list_of_types.addItemListener (this);
//                    clear list_of_types stimuli
// (accomplished by not adding to list_of_types)
 }                    // end of init response method

// ================================================================
//                    method that performs response for list_of_categ
 private void listOfCategResponse() {
   String selected_categ = list_of_categ.getSelectedItem();
//
//                    highlight selected_category
// (intrinsic to Choice component)
//                    display list_of_types for selected_category
   list_of_types.removeAll();
   if ("Living Room Furniture".equals(selected_categ)) {
     for (int i=0; i < living_rm_types.length; i++) {
       list_of_types.add (living_rm_types[i]);
     }
   }
   else if ("Dining Room Furniture".equals(selected_categ)) {
     for (int i=0; i < dining_rm_types.length; i++) {
       list_of_types.add (dining_rm_types[i]);
     }
   }
   else if ("Bedroom Furniture".equals(selected_categ)) {
     for (int i=0; i < bedrm_types.length; i++) {
       list_of_types.add (bedrm_types[i]);
     }
   }
   else if ("Office Furniture".equals(selected_categ)) {
     for (int i=0; i < office_types.length; i++) {
       list_of_types.add (office_types[i]);
     }
   }
//                    clear Furniture List SS stimuli
 }                    // end of list_of_categ response method
```

Listing 13.2   Functionality Module for Classification SS (continued)

```
// ===================================================================
//                  method that performs response for list_of_types
  private void listOfTypesResponse() {
    String selected_type = list_of_types.getSelectedItem();
//
//                  highlight selected_type
//                  activate Furniture List SS for selected_type

  }                 // end of list_of_types response method

}                   // end of module for stimulus set Classification
// ******************************************************************
```

Listing 13.3   Functionality Module for Mode SS

```
// ******************************************************************
//                  functionality module for SS Mode

package com.furmasco.inventory.gui;

import java.awt.Panel;
import java.awt.Checkbox;
import java.awt.CheckboxGroup;
import java.awt.event.ItemListener;
import java.awt.event.ItemEvent;

class Mode extends Panel implements ItemListener {

//                  data declarations for stimuli
  private Checkbox view;
  private Checkbox add;
  private Checkbox modify;

//                  data declarations for response behavior support
  private Inventory inventory_app;

// ******************************************************************
//                  Stimulus Methods
//
//                  activation method (constructor)
  public Mode () {
//                  save reference to main program
    inventory_app = Inventory.getInventory();

//                  create stimuli
    createStimuli();
//                  perform initialization response
    initResponse();
  }                 // end of activation method

// ===================================================================
```

Listing 13.3   Functionality Module for Mode SS (continued)

```
//                     method for creating stimuli of the stimulus set
   private void createStimuli() {
      CheckboxGroup cbg = new CheckboxGroup();
//                     create stimuli objects
      view = new Checkbox ("view", cbg, true);
      add = new Checkbox ("add", cbg, false);
      modify = new Checkbox ("modify", cbg, false);

//                     For human UIs, layout the stimuli look and feel
      layoutStimuli();
//                     enable list_of_furnories stimuli
      view.addItemListener (this);
      add.addItemListener (this);
      modify.addItemListener (this);
   }                   // end of method for creating stimuli

// =================================================================
//                     method for laying out an UI stimulus set
   private void layoutStimuli() {
//                     use default flow layout (horizontal centered)
      this.add (view);
      this.add (add);
      this.add (modify);
   }                   // end of method for  out an UI stimulus set

// =================================================================
//                     method for detecting stimulus events
   public void itemStateChanged (ItemEvent ie) {
      Object stimulus = ie.getSource();
      if (stimulus ==  view) {
         viewResponse();
      }
      else if (stimulus ==  add) {
         addResponse();
      }
      else if (stimulus ==  modify) {
         modifyResponse();
      }
   }                   // end of method for detecting stimulus events
// ****************************************************************
//                     Response Methods
//
//                     method that performs initialization response
   private void initResponse() {
//                     perform view response
      viewResponse();
   }                   // emd of init response method

// =================================================================
//                     method that performs response for view
   private void viewResponse() {
```

Listing 13.3   Functionality Module for Mode SS (continued)

```
      FurnitureData furn_data = inventory_app.getFurnitureData();
//                mark view stimulus as selected
//  (intrinsic to Checkbox component)
//                unmark add, modify stimuli
//  (intrinsic to CheckboxGroup component)
//                disable Furniture Data SS for input
      furn_data.disableStimuli();
   }                // end of view response method


// ==================================================================
//                method that performs response for add
   private void addResponse() {
      FurnitureData furn_data = inventory_app.getFurnitureData();
//                mark add stimulus as selected
//  (intrinsic to Checkbox component)
//                unmark view, modify stimuli
//  (intrinsic to CheckboxGroup component)
//                enable Furniture Data SS stimuli for input
      furn_data.enableStimuli();
   }                // end of add response method


// ==================================================================
//                method that performs response for modify
   private void modifyResponse() {
      FurnitureData furn_data = inventory_app.getFurnitureData();
//                mark modify stimulus as selected
//  (intrinsic to Checkbox component)
//                unmark view, add stimuli
//  (intrinsic to CheckboxGroup component)
//                enable Furniture Data SS quantity, price,
//                 select, reset for input
//                disable Furniture Data SS descrip, shipping wt,
//                 dimensions for input
      furn_data.enableStimuliForModify();
   }                // end of modify response method

}                   // end of module for stimulus set Mode
// ****************************************************************
```

Listing 13.4 Functionality Module for Inventory SS

```
// ****************************************************************
//                      functionality module for Inventory UI screen

package com.furmasco.inventory.gui;

import java.awt.Frame;
import java.awt.Panel;
import java.awt.BorderLayout;
import java.awt.GridLayout;
import java.awt.TextField;
import java.awt.event.WindowEvent;
import java.awt.event.WindowListener;

class Inventory extends Frame implements WindowListener {

//                      data declarations for stimuli
  private Classification classif;
  private FurnitureData furn_data;
  private FurnitureList furn_list;
  private Mode mode;

//                      data declarations for response behavior support
  private TextField msg_line;
  private static Inventory inventory_app;

// ****************************************************************
//                      Stimulus Methods
//
//                      activation method (constructor)
  public Inventory() {
    super ("Furmasco Furniture Inventory");
//                      save ref to the application
    inventory_app = this;
//                      create stimuli
    createStimuli();
//                      perform initialization response
    initResponse();
  }                       // end of activation method

// ================================================================
//                      method for creating stimuli of the stimulus set
  private void createStimuli() {
//                      create stimuli objects
    furn_data = new FurnitureData();
    furn_list = new FurnitureList();
    classif = new Classification();
    mode = new Mode();

    msg_line = new TextField (30);
    msg_line.setEnabled (false);

//                      For human UIs, layout the stimuli look and feel
    layoutStimulusSets();
```

Listing 13.4   Functionality Module for Inventory SS (continued)

```
//                 enable window stimuli
   this.addWindowListener (this);
 }                 // end of method for creating stimuli

// ==================================================================
//               method for laying out stimulus sets
 private void layoutStimulusSets() {
   Panel west_panel = new Panel (new BorderLayout());
   Panel south_panel = new Panel (new GridLayout(2,1));

   west_panel.add (classif, BorderLayout.NORTH);
   west_panel.add (furn_data, BorderLayout.SOUTH);

   south_panel.add (mode);
   south_panel.add (msg_line);

   this.add (west_panel, BorderLayout.WEST);
   this.add (furn_list, BorderLayout.CENTER);
   this.add (south_panel, BorderLayout.SOUTH);
 }                 // end of stimulus set layout method

// ==================================================================
//               methods for detecting window events

 public void windowActivated (WindowEvent we) {
 }

 public void windowClosed (WindowEvent we) {
 }

 public void windowClosing (WindowEvent we) {
   quitResponse();
 }

 public void windowDeactivated (WindowEvent we) {
 }

 public void windowIconified (WindowEvent we) {
 }

 public void windowDeiconified (WindowEvent we) {
 }

 public void windowOpened (WindowEvent we) {
 }
// end of methods for detecting window events

// ***************************************************************
//               Response Methods
//
//               method that performs initialization response
 private void initResponse() {
```

Listing 13.4   Functionality Module for Inventory SS (continued)

```
//                    display human interface screen
   this.pack();
   this.setVisible (true);
//                    activate Mode SS
//   (done when Mode created)
//                    activate Classification SS
//   (done when Classification created)

   }                  // end of init response method

// ================================================================
//                    method that performs response for quit
   private void quitResponse() {
//                    exit program
   this.dispose();
   System.exit(0);
   }                  // end of quit response method

// ****************************************************************
//                    Access Methods
//
//                    method for getting Inventory program reference
   public static Inventory getInventory() {
     return Inventory.inventory_app;
   }                  // end of Inventory program getter method

// ================================================================
//                    method for getting Classification SS reference
   public Classification getClassification() {
     return this.classif;
   }                  // end of Classification SS getter method

// ================================================================
//                    method for getting FurnitureData SS reference
   public FurnitureData getFurnitureData() {
     return this.furn_data;
   }                  // end of FurnitureData SS getter method

// ================================================================
//                    method for getting FurnitureList SS reference
   public FurnitureList getFurnitureList() {
     return this.furn_list;
   }          .       // end of FurnitureList SS getter method

// ================================================================
//                    method for getting Mode SS reference
   public Mode getMode() {
     return this.mode;
   }                  // end of Mode SS getter method

// ================================================================
```

Listing 13.4 Functionality Module for Inventory SS (continued)

```
//                 method for getting message line reference
  public TextField getMessageLine() {
    return this.msg_line;
  }                    // end of message line getter method


// *******************************************************************
//                       Main Method
//
//                 main method of Inventory program
  public static void main (String[] args) {
    new Inventory();
  }                    // end of main method

}                      // end of module for Inventory UI screen
// *******************************************************************
```

References

1. Floyd, C. ca.1984. A systematic look at prototyping. *Institut for Angewandte Informatik*, TU Berlin Sekr. SWT FR5-6.

Chapter 14

Requirements Evolution

14.1 Chapter Overview

This chapter examines the Freedom requirements change process. Requirements can change at anytime in the life of the software from initial development through post-delivery evolution. At some points in the life cycle, explicit plans are made for requirements change. The first such point is during customer evaluation of the requirements prototype, as illustrated in Figure 14.1. Regardless of when requirements change occurs, the general Freedom process for dealing with it is the same. Variations in the process occur based on the scope of the change and the degree of completion of the software.

14.2 Handling the Ripple Effect of Change

A requirements change may take one of three forms:

1. A change to a stimulus (functionality tree),
2. A change to an external response (behavior table), or
3. A change to a protocol (functionality screen or programmatic protocol specification).

Each of these possibilities is discussed in the following sections.

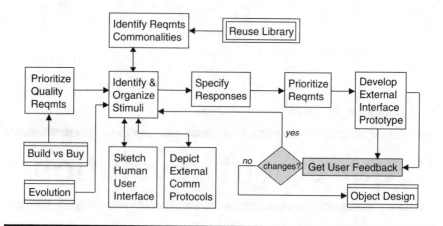

Figure 14.1   Requirements verification in the requirements process.

14.2.1 Ripple Effect of Stimulus Change

At the requirements level, a change to a stimulus usually results in a change to its associated response and its implementing protocol. If a stimulus is added or deleted, its external response and implementing protocol object will also be added or deleted. If a stimulus is modified, such as by a name change, its response may be unaffected but its implementing protocol manifestation will usually change.

Figure 14.2 illustrates the dependencies among the three requirements notations (functionality tree, functionality screen, and behavior table) and their implementing source code. The dependencies are denoted by arrows. The numbers on the arrows represent the sequence of propagation of the ripple effect of a stimulus change through the software system.

Dependency 1. Stimulus Changes in Protocol and Functionality Tree

A stimulus change is typically initiated by users in the form of a request for a change to an external protocol such as a human interface or programmatic command-data stream. The developer or maintainer updates the stimuli in the functionality tree to be consistent with the requested protocol change.

Dependency 2. Stimulus Change Propagates to Behavior Table

If the stimulus change is a simple name change, the name of the stimulus is changed in the behavior table for the stimulus set. The response behavior is unaffected.

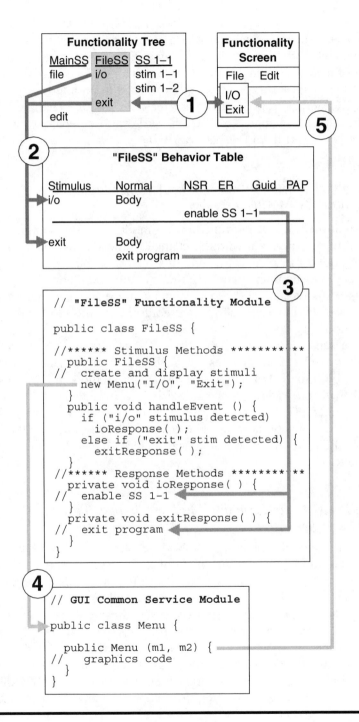

Figure 14.2   Ripple effect of stimulus change.

If the stimulus change is an addition (i.e., a new stimulus), a row is added to the behavior table for the stimulus. The users or customer representatives are consulted regarding the required external response behavior for the new stimulus, and the behavior entered into the behavior table. If the change is to a release, as opposed to an interface prototype, associated internal response behavior may also require change.

If the stimulus change is a deletion, the response behavior row for the stimulus is deleted from the behavior table.

Dependency 3. Stimulus–Response Change Propagates to Functionality Module

The stimuli methods of the functionality module for the stimulus set are modified to be consistent with the change to the stimulus. If the stimulus is being added or deleted, the stimulus methods will create or delete a corresponding stimulus object. If the stimulus is being changed, the stimulus methods are modified to change the external manifestation of the stimulus. In all cases, the change conforms to the modified protocol specification.

At the same time, a corresponding change is made to the response methods to reflect the changes to the behavior table. This will involve changing both the event handler or dispatcher method, and the response method that encapsulates the external behavior of the specific stimulus being changed. The "3" arrow in Figure 14.2 explicitly shows only one aspect of these functionality module changes, namely, copying the behavior table PDL to the response encapsulation method in the form of comments.

Dependency 4. Functionality Module Changes Propagate to Common Services

Changes to both the stimulus methods and response methods of the functionality module can result in changes to common service modules.

In the case of the stimulus methods, different common services may need to be invoked to present the new external protocol view specified by the protocol specification. In most cases, these common services will be reusable libraries and no common service code will actually need to be written, but rather used in a different manner.

In the case of the response methods, some of the common service changes may involve using reusable design libraries in a slightly different manner. Other changes may require altering common service module code, such as changes to "business logic" corresponding to modified internal response behavior.

Note that coding changes to common services will usually involve performing one or more tasks of the Object Design process. Details of the Object Design process of Freedom are beyond the scope of this book.

Dependency 5. Common Service Changes Propagate to External Protocol

This dependency does not involve any work on the part of the developer or maintainer. The "5" arrow in Figure 14.2 simply indicates that the externally visible changes at runtime resulting from the above modifications are usually directly attributable to common services, particularly reusable common service libraries for protocols such as graphics, networking, and other forms of input/output.

14.2.2 Ripple Effect of External Response Change

At the requirements level, a change to an external response should not affect the associated stimulus. However, the implementing protocol may or may not change.

Figure 14.3 illustrates the dependencies among the relevant requirements notation (behavior table) and its implementing source code. The dependencies are denoted by arrows. The numbers on the arrows represent the sequence of propagation of the ripple effect of a response change through the software system.

Dependency 1. Response Change Propagates to Functionality Module

A response change is typically initiated by users in the form of a request for a change to the external behavior of some stimulus projected from either a human or programmatic interface. The developer or maintainer updates the response in the behavior table of the appropriate stimulus set to be consistent with the user request.

The stimuli methods of the functionality module for the stimulus set will usually be unaffected. However, the behavior encapsulating response method for the stimulus is modified based on the change to the behavior table. The "1" arrow in Figure 14.3 explicitly shows only one aspect of the response method change, namely, copying the changed behavior table PDL to the response encapsulation method in the form of comments.

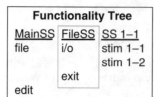

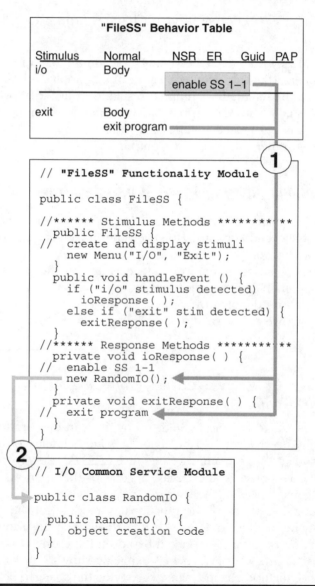

Figure 14.3   Ripple effect of external response change.

Dependency 2. Functionality Module Changes Propagate to Common Services

Changes to response methods of the functionality module can result in changes to common service modules, particularly when internal behavior changes along with external (requirements) behavior in the behavior table.

Some common service changes propagating from response method changes may involve using reusable design libraries in a slightly different manner. Other changes may require altering application-specific common service code, such as changes to "business logic" corresponding to modified internal response behavior.

Note that coding changes to common services will usually involve performing one or more tasks of the Object Design process, which for Freedom, as mentioned above, is beyond the scope of this book.

14.2.3 Ripple Effect of Protocol Change

From the standpoint of requirements, a change to an implementing protocol should have no effect on the stimulus because the functionality tree should be implementation neutral. The response should also be unaffected because PDL references to specific protocol features should be rare. For graphical interfaces, the change may involve use of a different type of component, say a slider instead of a text entry field, a different color or font, or a different arrangement of the stimulus sets, to name a few possibilities. For programmatic interfaces, the change may involve a different carrier standard, such as a synchronous instead of an asynchronous protocol, or an error-correcting protocol instead of a noncorrecting protocol. If the protocol change *does* have an effect on the functionality tree or behavior table, one of the above two cases (stimulus change or response change) applies; that is, it is not a protocol-only change.

Figure 14.4 illustrates the dependencies among the relevant requirements notation (functionality screen) and its implementing source code. The dependencies are denoted by arrows. The numbers on the arrows represent the sequence of propagation of the ripple effect of a protocol-only change through the software system.

Dependency 1. Protocol Change Propagates to Functionality Module

A protocol change is typically initiated by users in the form of a request for a change to a human interface, or to a programmatic stream to an external system or the environment. The developer or maintainer updates

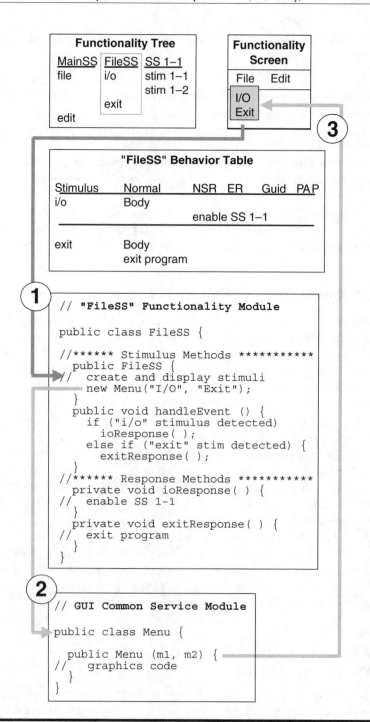

Figure 14.4   Ripple effect of protocol change.

the functionality screen or other protocol specification consistent with the user request. The stimuli creation methods of the appropriate functionality module are then modified to be consistent with the change to the protocol.

Dependency 2. Functionality Module Changes Propagate to Common Services

The change to the stimulus creation methods will usually necessitate that different common services be invoked to present the external protocol view specified by the revised protocol specification. In most cases, these common services will be reusable libraries. No common service code will actually need to be written, but rather used in a different manner.

Dependency 3. Common Service Changes Propagate to External Protocol

This dependency does not involve any work on the part of the developer or maintainer. The "3" arrow in Figure 14.4 simply indicates that the externally visible changes at runtime resulting from the above modifications are usually directly attributable to common services, particularly reusable common service libraries for protocols such as graphics, networking, and other forms of input/output.

14.3 Requirements Change Example

At the shipping department staff meeting, all shipping personnel are instructed to exercise the external interface mockup prototype and submit their comments and suggestions to the development team within two days. The "hollow shell" nature of the prototype is made clear to all employees, as is the need to pay special attention to missing or incorrect functionality as exhibited by the external interface components. Participation is good. Members of the development team are available to answer questions and provide explanations of intended response behavior of the software during the trial runs. Two days later the development team sorts through the results.

> Shipping, Lead: Feedback on the prototype is very good. No one thinks any existing features are unnecessary. There are a few suggestions for additional input options.
>
> IT: The most requested new thing is various sort options for the list of furniture data.

Shipping: A lot of comments about the look and feel, too. Everyone thought that making everything white was too stark. Most thought the company colors and logo would make it look more presentable.

IT: There is another pile of comments here about the arrangement. Some thought the list of furniture should be on top and not to the side.

Shipping, Lead: These are good ideas, and we should update the requirements to include them all. Priority should go to the suggestions that are most relevant to the initial "data entry" release.

IT: Right. That means we can defer sort selection stimuli. Those will be useful for quarterly statistical reporting and stuff, but not really needed for the initial data entry.

Shipping: I agree. Some of the users I talked to said they couldn't stand the all-white appearance, and a lot of them made a big deal about the entry fields being to one side instead of centered under the furniture list window. Maybe it's just aesthetics, but that can be important for those who will be spending eight hours a day doing data entry.

Shipping, Lead: I agree. We should implement the color change suggestions, and the new layout.

IT: I'm not sure about the layout. A lot of the users I talked to commented on how nice the current layout is. I think they liked it the way it is. If we change it, we may make these users upset.

Shipping, Lead: Hmm. . . . There are only 15 people in the department, so maybe we should just go ask them. Let's come up with a functionality screen with the furniture list on top, then show each user the old and proposed new screen drawings side by side and see what the majority prefer.

IT: Good idea. Otherwise, we could go in circles forever with aesthetics issues.

The team quickly creates a functionality screen with the furniture list at the top. The team members then survey the user's opinions on the old versus new functionality screens. A couple of hours later the team meets to compare notes.

Shipping, Lead: Well, here are the totals, and guess what?

IT: 50–50?

Shipping, Lead: You got it! Six for the old layout and seven for the new one. I personally talked to the department manager. He didn't give a preference, but just said to make everyone happy.

Shipping: Great! Big help!!

IT: Well, maybe we *can* make everyone happy. How about this?

He takes his copy of the two functionality screens and draws a single new button on each one. The result looks like Listings 14.1 and 14.2.

IT: Toggle this new checkbox called Vert Layout and the screen automatically flips between the old and new layouts. So the user can select whichever arrangement she prefers.

Shipping: Can you do that?

IT 2: With Java, sure—shouldn't be too hard.

IT 1: In fact, we just happened to do a quality requirements type trade-off that included exactly this capability. Look at Listing 13.2 in our notes. The prototype code is actually designed to support multiple layouts.

Shipping, Lead: Well, then that's the answer. Go for it!

*   *   *

The IT team members start the revision to the external interface mockup by noting the change involves addition of a new stimulus, and so involves five steps:

1. Promulgate the functionality screen change into the functionality tree.
2. Update the behavior table for the new stimulus.

Listing 14.1   Inventory Revised Functionality Screen, "List Right"

```
---------------------------------------------------------------------
|               Furmasco Furniture Inventory              Quit |
|-------------------------------------------------------------------|
|   Furniture Classification        |        List of Furniture       |
|                                   |                              __|
|   --------------------            |  XXX XXXXXXXXXXXXXXXXXXXXXX  |^||
|   | <classif categ>  |^|          |  XXX XXXXXXXXXXXXXXXXXXXXXX  |_||
|   --------------------            |  XXX XXXXXXXXXXXXXXXXXXXXXX  |-||
|   --------------------            |  XXX XXXXXXXXXXXXXXXXXXXXXX  | ||
|   | Select Type      |^|          |  XXX XXXXXXXXXXXXXXXXXXXXXX  | ||
|   --------------------            |  XXX XXXXXXXXXXXXXXXXXXXXXX  | ||
|-----------------------------------|  XXX XXXXXXXXXXXXXXXXXXXXXX  | ||
|        Furniture Data             |  XXX XXXXXXXXXXXXXXXXXXXXXX  | ||
|                _____   |  XXX XXXXXXXXXXXXXXXXXXXXXX  | ||
|    Descrip   |_____|   |  XXX XXXXXXXXXXXXXXXXXXXXXX  | ||
|                _____            |  XXX XXXXXXXXXXXXXXXXXXXXXX  | ||
|    Quantity  |_____|           |  XXX XXXXXXXXXXXXXXXXXXXXXX  | ||
|                _____              |  XXX XXXXXXXXXXXXXXXXXXXXXX  | ||
|      Price   |_____|             |  XXX XXXXXXXXXXXXXXXXXXXXXX  | ||
|                _____              |  XXX XXXXXXXXXXXXXXXXXXXXXX  | ||
|    Ship Wt   |_____|             |  XXX XXXXXXXXXXXXXXXXXXXXXX  | ||
|                _____        |  XXX XXXXXXXXXXXXXXXXXXXXXX  | ||
|  Dimensions  |_w,_h,_d__|         |  XXX XXXXXXXXXXXXXXXXXXXXXX  | ||
|       _____    _____         |  XXX XXXXXXXXXXXXXXXXXXXXXX  | ||
|      | Select |  | Reset  |       |  XXX XXXXXXXXXXXXXXXXXXXXXX  | ||
|       --------    --------         |  XXX XXXXXXXXXXXXXXXXXXXXXX  |v||
|-------------------------------------------------------------------|
|           <x> View    < > Add    < > Modify                       |
|                    < > Vert Layout                                |
|-------------------------------------------------------------------|
| message area                                                      |
---------------------------------------------------------------------
```

3. Modify the functionality module code for the new stimulus–response requirement.
4. Modify any common service code affected by the functionality module changes.
5. Rerun the program and observe that the protocol and behavior changes are implemented correctly.

Dependency 1. Stimulus Changes in Protocol and Functionality Tree

The requested change involves addition of the Vert Layout stimulus, which causes the layout of the stimulus sets on the screen to change. As noted previously, the layout change is drawn as two functionality screens, as shown in Listings 14.1 and 14.2.

The IT development team members quickly update the functionality tree with the Vert Layout stimulus, which is part of the Mode stimulus

Listing 14.2   Inventory Revised Functionality Screen, "List Top"

```
 -------------------------------------------------------------------
|                 Furmasco Furniture Inventory          Quit |
|-----------------------------------------------------------------|
|                       List of Furniture                         |
|                                                              __ |
|  xxx xxxxxxxxxxxxxxxxxxxxxxxxxxxxxxxxxxxxxxxxxxxxxxxxxxxxxx  |^| |
|  xxx xxxxxxxxxxxxxxxxxxxxxxxxxxxxxxxxxxxxxxxxxxxxxxxxxxxxxx  |-| |
|  xxx xxxxxxxxxxxxxxxxxxxxxxxxxxxxxxxxxxxxxxxxxxxxxxxxxxxxxx  | | |
|  xxx xxxxxxxxxxxxxxxxxxxxxxxxxxxxxxxxxxxxxxxxxxxxxxxxxxxxxx  | | |
|  xxx xxxxxxxxxxxxxxxxxxxxxxxxxxxxxxxxxxxxxxxxxxxxxxxxxxxxxx  | | |
|  xxx xxxxxxxxxxxxxxxxxxxxxxxxxxxxxxxxxxxxxxxxxxxxxxxxxxxxxx  | | |
|  xxx xxxxxxxxxxxxxxxxxxxxxxxxxxxxxxxxxxxxxxxxxxxxxxxxxxxxxx  | | |
|  xxx xxxxxxxxxxxxxxxxxxxxxxxxxxxxxxxxxxxxxxxxxxxxxxxxxxxxxx  | | |
|  xxx xxxxxxxxxxxxxxxxxxxxxxxxxxxxxxxxxxxxxxxxxxxxxxxxxxxxxx  | | |
|  xxx xxxxxxxxxxxxxxxxxxxxxxxxxxxxxxxxxxxxxxxxxxxxxxxxxxxxxx  |v| |
|-------------------------------------------------------------|   |
|  Furniture Classification   |         Furniture Data          |
|                             |                                 |
|   --------------------      |          _____       |
|  | <classif categ> |^|      |   Descrip |_____|   |
|   --------------------      |           _____            |
|   --------------------      |  Quantity |_____|           |
|  | Select Type     |^|      |           _____            |
|   --------------------      |     Price |_____|           |
|-------------------------------|         _____            |
|                             |   Ship Wt |_____|           |
|  <x> View  < > Add  < > Modify |        _____            |
|                             | Dimensions  |__w,_h,_d__|     |
|                             |           _____      _____   |
|         <x> Vert Layout     |          | Select |  | Reset |  |
|                             |           --------    --------  |
|-------------------------------------------------------------|
| message area                                                |
 -------------------------------------------------------------------
```

set. Because the team agreed that the stimulus was relevant to the high-priority "data entry" user task, they highlight the new stimulus in the functionality tree to indicate it is high priority and part of the initial release. The modified functionality tree appears in Listing 14.3.

Dependency 2. Stimulus Change Propagates to Behavior Table

Prior to recording the response for the new stimulus, the IT team members enlist the assistance of one of the shipping team members because shipping is the primary customer for the inventory system. Together, the shipping and IT development team members specify the external response for the Vert Layout stimulus by adding a new row in the Mode SS behavior table. They also update the initialization response as it pertains to the new stimulus. The updated behavior table is shown in Listing 14.4.

Listing 14.3   Inventory Revised Functionality Tree

```
Level 0            Level 1
Inventory SS
quit

Classification SS  Furniture List SS
list of types          list of furniture

list of categ

Mode SS            Furniture Data SS
add                    description
                       quantity
                       price
                       shipping wt
                       dimensions
                       select
                       reset

                   Furniture Data SS
modify                 (reused SS)
view
vert layout

Notes:
1. to delete, modify with negative quantity
2. stimulus -- highest priority
```

Dependency 3. Stimulus–Response Change Propagates to Functionality Module

With the new Vert Layout requirement (stimulus–response) specified, the functionality modules of the interface mockup are modified. Two functionality modules are affected. The first is the Mode class, which implements the ModeSS stimulus set. The stimulus methods are updated by adding a new checkbox for the Vert Layout stimulus. Also, a new response method, called vLayoutResponse(), is added to encapsulate the Vert Layout response specified in the behavior table. As usual, the PDL for the Vert Layout response is copied from the behavior table to the vLayoutResponse() method as comments, and each line of implementing code placed below its authorizing PDL. The modified Mode class is given in Listing 14.5.

The Vert Layout response code simply calls one of the two layout methods in the Inventory class. The "horizontal" (furniture list on right) layout method already exists in the mockup, but the method for the "vertical" (furniture list on top) layout needs to be written. Thus, the Inventory class is also updated by writing a method called layoutStimulusSetsVert() for the Inventory class. For clarity, the name of the original

Listing 14.4 Inventory Revised Human Interface "Mode" Behavior Table

```
Behavior Table for Inventory Human User Mode SS
                                        D & I        D & I
Stimulus  Normal    NSR       Error     Constraint  Guidance  PAP
--------  --------  --------  --------  ----------  --------  --------
init    * Output
        *   vertical_layout_mode
            Body
        * clear vertical_layout_mode
        * perform vert layout response
            perform view response
--------  --------  --------  --------  ----------  --------  --------
view      Body
          mark view stimulus as selected
          unmark add, modify stimuli
                  disable Furniture Data SS for input
--------  --------  --------  --------  ----------  --------  --------
add       Body
          mark add stimulus as selected
          unmark view, modify stimuli
                  enable Furniture Data SS stimuli for input
--------  --------  --------  --------  ----------  --------  --------
modify    Body
          mark modify stimulus as selected
          unmark view, add stimuli
                  enable Furniture Data SS quantity, price,
                  select, reset for input
                  disable Furniture Data SS descrip, shipping wt,
                  dimensions for input
--------  --------  --------  --------  ----------  --------  --------
vert    * Input
layout  *   vertical_layout_mode
        * Body
        * invert mark of vert layout stimulus
        * invert vertical_layout_mode
        * IF vertical_layout_mode set
        * THEN
        *   arrange SS in vertical layout
        * ELSE
        *   arrange SS in horizontal layout
        * END IF
--------  --------  --------  --------  ----------  --------  --------

Notes:
* = added by revision due to prototype feedback
```

layout method layoutStimulusSets() is changed to layoutStimulusSetsHoriz(). The code for the modified Inventory class is given in Listing 14.6.

Note that it is acceptable to change the name of the layoutStimulusSets() method because, like most stimulus methods, it is access-restricted, and is not part of the public stable interface of the class. That is, the stimulus and response (requirements-implementing) methods are encapsulated, meaning they are free to change when the requirement they implement

Listing 14.5   Revised Functionality Module for Mode SS

```
// ********************************************************************
//                    functionality module for SS Mode

package com.furmasco.inventory.gui;

import java.awt.Panel;
import java.awt.Checkbox;
import java.awt.CheckboxGroup;
import java.awt.GridLayout;
import java.awt.event.ItemListener;
import java.awt.event.ItemEvent;

class Mode extends Panel implements ItemListener {

//                    data declarations for stimuli
  private Checkbox view;
  private Checkbox add;
  private Checkbox modify;
  private Checkbox v_layout;

//                    data declarations for response behavior support
  private Inventory inventory_app;

// ********************************************************************
//                    Stimulus Methods
//
//                    activation method (constructor)
  public Mode () {
//                    save reference to main program
    inventory_app = Inventory.getInventory();

//                    create stimuli
    createStimuli();
//                    perform initialization response
    initResponse();
  }                   // end of activation method

// ================================================================
//                    method for creating stimuli of the stimulus set
  private void createStimuli() {
    CheckboxGroup cbg = new CheckboxGroup();
//                    create stimuli objects
    view = new Checkbox ("view", cbg, true);
    add = new Checkbox ("add", cbg, false);
    modify = new Checkbox ("modify", cbg, false);
    v_layout = new Checkbox ("Vert Layout", false);

//                    For human UIs, layout the stimuli look and feel
    layoutStimuli();
//                    enable list_of_furnories stimuli
    view.addItemListener (this);
    add.addItemListener (this);
    modify.addItemListener (this);
    v_layout.addItemListener (this);
```

Listing 14.5   Revised Functionality Module for Mode SS (continued)

```
  }                    // end of method for creating stimuli

// ==================================================================
//                  method for laying out an UI stimulus set
  private void layoutStimuli() {
    Panel cbg_panel = new Panel();
    Panel vl_panel = new Panel();

    cbg_panel.add (view);
    cbg_panel.add (add);
    cbg_panel.add (modify);

    vl_panel.add (v_layout);

    this.setLayout (new GridLayout(2,1));
    this.add (cbg_layout);
    this.add (vl_panel);
  }                    // end of method for  out an UI stimulus set

// ==================================================================
//                  method for detecting stimulus events
  public void itemStateChanged (ItemEvent ie) {
    Object stimulus = ie.getSource();
    if (stimulus ==  view) {
      viewResponse();
    }
    else if (stimulus ==  add) {
      addResponse();
    }
    else if (stimulus ==  modify) {
      modifyResponse();
    }
    else if (stimulus ==  v_layout) {
      vLayoutResponse();
    }
  }                    // end of method for detecting stimulus events

// ******************************************************************
//                  Response Methods
//
//                  method that performs initialization response
  private void initResponse() {
//                  clear vertical_layout_mode
//  (handled by Inventory stimuli methods)
//                  perform horiz layout response
//  (handled by Inventory stimuli methods)
//                  perform view response
    viewResponse();
  }                    // emd of init response method

// ==================================================================
```

Listing 14.5   Revised Functionality Module for Mode SS (continued)

```
//                      method that performs response for view
  private void viewResponse() {
    FurnitureData furn_data = inventory_app.getFurnitureData();
//                      mark view stimulus as selected
//  (intrinsic to Checkbox component)
//                      unmark add, modify stimuli
//  (intrinsic to CheckboxGroup component)
//                      disable Furniture Data SS for input
    furn_data.disableStimuli();
  }                     // end of view response method

// ===================================================================
//                      method that performs response for add
  private void addResponse() {
    FurnitureData furn_data = inventory_app.getFurnitureData();
//                      mark add stimulus as selected
//  (intrinsic to Checkbox component)
//                      unmark view, modify stimuli
//  (intrinsic to CheckboxGroup component)
//                      enable Furniture Data SS stimuli for input
    furn_data.enableStimuli();
  }                     // end of add response method

// ===================================================================
//                      method that performs response for modify
  private void modifyResponse() {
    FurnitureData furn_data = inventory_app.getFurnitureData();
//                      mark modify stimulus as selected
//  (intrinsic to Checkbox component)
//                      unmark view, add stimuli
//  (intrinsic to CheckboxGroup component)
//                      enable Furniture Data SS quantity, price,
//                       select, reset for input
//                      disable Furniture Data SS descrip, shipping wt,
//                       dimensions for input
    furn_data.enableStimuliForModify();
  }                     // end of modify response method

// ===================================================================
//                      method that performs response for modify
  private void vLayoutResponse() {
//                      invert mark of vert_layout stimulus
//  (intrinsic to Checkbox component)
//                      invert vertical_layout_mode
//  (intrinsic to Checkbox component)
//                      IF vertical_layout_mode set
    if (v_layout.getState()) {
//                      THEN
//                        arrange SS in vertical layout
      inventory_app.layoutStimulusSetsVert();
//                      ELSE
    }
    else {
```

Listing 14.5 Revised Functionality Module for Mode SS (continued)

```
//                      arrange SS in horizontal layout
      inventory_app.layoutStimulusSetsHoriz();
//                      END IF
      }
  }                     // end of modify response method

}                       // end of module for stimulus set Mode
// ****************************************************************
```

Listing 14.6 Revised Functionality Module for Inventory SS

```
// ****************************************************************
//                    functionality module for Inventory UI screen

package com.furmasco.inventory.gui;

import java.awt.Frame;
import java.awt.Panel;
import java.awt.BorderLayout;
import java.awt.GridLayout;
import java.awt.TextField;
import java.awt.event.WindowEvent;
import java.awt.event.WindowListener;

class Inventory extends Frame implements WindowListener {

//                    data declarations for stimuli
  private Classification classif;
  private FurnitureData furn_data;
  private FurnitureList furn_list;
  private Mode mode;
  private Panel south_panel = new Panel();
  private Panel west_panel = new Panel();

//                    data declarations for response behavior support
  private TextField msg_line;
  private static Inventory inventory_app;

// ****************************************************************
//                    Stimulus Methods
//
//                    activation method (constructor)
  public Inventory() {
    super ("Furmasco Furniture Inventory");
//                    save ref to the application
    inventory_app = this;
//                    create stimuli
    createStimuli();
//                    perform initialization response
    initResponse();
  }                     // end of activation method
```

Listing 14.6 Revised Functionality Module for Inventory SS (continued)

```
// ================================================================
//                  method for creating stimuli of the stimulus set
  private void createStimuli() {
//                  create stimuli objects
     furn_data = new FurnitureData();
     furn_list = new FurnitureList();
     classif = new Classification();
     mode = new Mode();

     msg_line = new TextField (30);
     msg_line.setEnabled (false);

//                  For human UIs, layout the stimuli look and feel
     layoutStimulusSetsHoriz();

//                  enable window stimuli
     this.addWindowListener (this);
  }                 // end of method for creating stimuli

// ================================================================
//                  method for laying out stimulus sets horizontally
  protected void layoutStimulusSetsHoriz() {
     west_panel.removeAll();
     south_panel.removeAll();
     this.removeAll();
     this.invalidate();

     west_panel.setLayout (new BorderLayout());
     south_panel.setLayout (new BorderLayout());

     west_panel.add (classif, BorderLayout.NORTH);
     west_panel.add (furn_data, BorderLayout.SOUTH);

     south_panel.add (mode, BorderLayout.CENTER);
     south_panel.add (msg_line, BorderLayout.SOUTH);

     this.add (west_panel, BorderLayout.WEST);
     this.add (furn_list, BorderLayout.CENTER);
     this.add (south_panel, BorderLayout.SOUTH);

     this.validate();
  }                 // end of stimulus set layout method

// ================================================================
//                  method for laying out stimulus sets vertically
  protected void layoutStimulusSetsVert() {
     west_panel.removeAll();
     south_panel.removeAll();
     this.removeAll();
     this.invalidate();

     south_panel.setLayout (new BorderLayout());
     west_panel.setLayout (new GridLayout(2,1));
```

Listing 14.6   Revised Functionality Module for Inventory SS (continued)

```
   west_panel.add (classif);
   west_panel.add (mode);

   south_panel.add (west_panel, BorderLayout.WEST);
   south_panel.add (furn_data, BorderLayout.EAST);
   south_panel.add (msg_line, BorderLayout.SOUTH);

   this.add (furn_list, BorderLayout.CENTER);
   this.add (south_panel, BorderLayout.SOUTH);

   this.validate();
  }                  // end of stimulus set layout method

// ==================================================================
//                   methods for detecting window events

  public void windowActivated (WindowEvent we) {
  }

  public void windowClosed (WindowEvent we) {
  }

  public void windowClosing (WindowEvent we) {
    quitResponse();
  }

  public void windowDeactivated (WindowEvent we) {
  }

  public void windowIconified (WindowEvent we) {
  }

  public void windowDeiconified (WindowEvent we) {
  }

  public void windowOpened (WindowEvent we) {
  }
// end of methods for detecting window events

// ******************************************************************
//                   Response Methods
//
//                   method that performs initialization response
  private void initResponse() {
//                   display human interface screen
    this.pack();
    this.setVisible (true);
//                   activate Mode SS
//  (done when Mode created)
//                   activate Classification SS
//  (done when Classification created)

  }                  // end of init response method
```

Listing 14.6   Revised Functionality Module for Inventory SS (continued)

```
// ===================================================================
//                  method that performs response for quit
  private void quitResponse() {
//                  exit program
    this.dispose();
    System.exit(0);
  }                  // end of quit response method

// *******************************************************************
//                  Access Methods
//
//                  method for getting Inventory program reference
  public static Inventory getInventory() {
    return Inventory.inventory_app;
  }                  // end of Inventory program getter method

// ===================================================================
//                  method for getting Classification SS reference
  public Classification getClassification() {
    return this.classif;
  }                  // end of Classification SS getter method

// ===================================================================
//                  method for getting FurnitureData SS reference
  public FurnitureData getFurnitureData() {
    return this.furn_data;
  }                  // end of FurnitureData SS getter method

// ===================================================================
//                  method for getting FurnitureList SS reference
  public FurnitureList getFurnitureList() {
    return this.furn_list;
  }                  // end of FurnitureList SS getter method

// ===================================================================
//                  method for getting Mode SS reference
  public Mode getMode() {
    return this.mode;
  }                  // end of Mode SS getter method

// ===================================================================
//                  method for getting message line reference
  public TextField getMessageLine() {
    return this.msg_line;
  }                  // end of message line getter method

// *******************************************************************
//                  Main Method
//
//                  main method of Inventory program
  public static void main (String[] args) {
    new Inventory();
```

Listing 14.6   Revised Functionality Module for Inventory SS (continued)

```
    }                      // end of main method

}                          // end of module for Inventory UI screen
//  ***********************************************************************
```

changes without undue propagation of ripple effects throughout the program.

Dependency 4. Functionality Module Changes Propagate to Common Services

Because this is a prototype, there are no internal responses and, therefore, no common service modules implementing internal behavior such as "business logic" to be changed. The only common services affected are classes and methods of the reusable Java GUI toolkit used by the stimulus creation methods. The new Vert Layout requirement causes additional calls to be made to the GUI toolkit, but the reusable GUI methods themselves do not change. Therefore, the requirements change to the mockup does not propagate into the code of any common service modules.

Dependency 5. Common Service Changes Propagate to External Protocol

As a final step, the IT team members rerun the modified external interface mockup prototype to verify conformance to the updated functionality screen and behavior tables, and to ensure bug-free operation. After fixing a few minor coding errors, the mockup runs perfectly; toggling the Vert Layout checkbox causes an immediate flip to the alternate layout. The IT team members make a screen shot of the "as built" screen for entry into their development notebook. The two screen shots are shown in Figures 14.5 and 14.6.

*   *   *

As the above requirements change example makes clear, the requirements work products—functionality tree, functionality screens, and behavior tables—play an integral part in the software maintenance process. Therefore, these work products should be archived along with the code, and kept current as the code is changed in response to new or changed requirements.

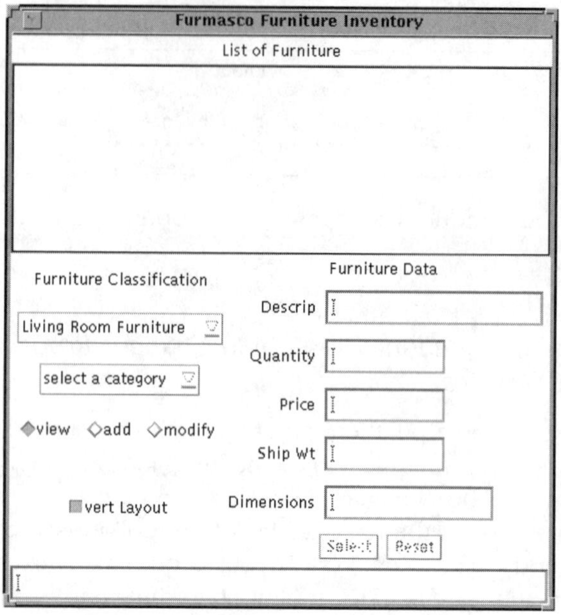

Figure 14.5   Inventory external interface mockup screen shot, "List Top."

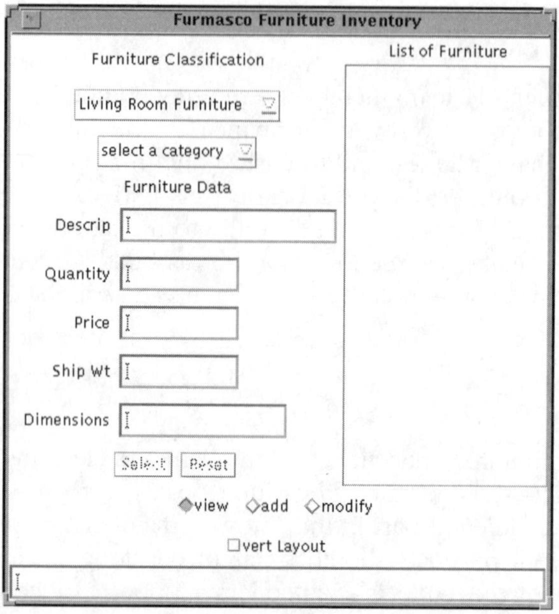

Figure 14.6   Inventory external interface mockup screen shot, "List Right."

Appendix A

Software Requirements Specification

This appendix is a sample template for a Software Requirements Specification (SRS) for projects that use Freedom and also wish to produce formal requirements documentation.

Table of Contents

1 Introduction and Overview

An overview of the problem to be solved and the software system intended to solve it. Natural language descriptions of the software system, that often pose as "requirements" for some projects, may be included in this section. From the black box model perspective, such information merely provides a useful introduction to the real requirements, that is, a specification of the external interface of the software system. Any such natural language descriptions should be kept short and high-level, consistent with their role as an overview of the system.

2 Context Diagram

The highest-level external view of the software system. The context diagram identifies all actors that interact with the software system including human users, external systems, and environmental stimulus sources. Arrows between the actors and the software system identify the external interfaces to the system. Labels on the arrows identify major inputs and outputs that flow across the interface.

3 Quality Requirements

The ranked quality attributes for the project are listed. If the ranking differs from the default ranking, an explanation of the variances can provide valuable insight into the customer's priorities for software quality.

4 Functionality Tree

The complete functionality tree that identifies and organizes the system stimuli, identifies reusable and repetitive stimulus sets, and prioritizes the stimuli into release groups. The functionality tree may be broken into parts for printing and display purposes. If this is done, each part appears in a subsection such as human, external system, and environment interface functionality trees.

4.1 Human Interface Functionality Tree

4.2 External System Interface Functionality Tree

4.3 Environment Interface Functionality Tree

5 Behavior Tables

One table per stimulus set that specifies the normal, NSR, error, and PAP response to each stimulus. Notes can appear below each table, as necessary. Internal response columns, including D&I constraints and guidance, will ideally be blank in a requirements specification. If the functionality tree is broken into parts that appear in separate subsections, the behavior tables should appear in corresponding subsections.

5.1 Human Interface Behavior Tables

5.2 External System Interface Behavior Tables

5.3 Environment Interface Behavior Tables

6 Protocols

Details of the programmatic protocols by which the stimuli will be projected to the actors or external environment. They may be organized into subchapters based on external sources such as human user (functionality screens), external systems, environment, and external files or external databases.

6.1 Functionality Screens

6.2 External System Programmatic Protocols

6.3 Environment Programmatic Protocols

6.4 File I/O Protocols

7 Glossary

An alphabetical listing of definitions for application-specific terminology used in the other sections of the SRS.

Appendix A.A Customer Enterprise Process Chart

The portion of the customer enterprise process chart (i.e., enterprise model or mission model) that defines the boundaries of the software system black box and serves as the basis for the context diagram.

Appendix A.B Prototype Source Code

The source code for the interface mockup requirements prototype.

Appendix B

Cost Savings Estimate Details

This appendix describes in detail the equations used to estimate life-cycle cost savings of the Freedom approach to requirements. Most importantly, it also describes the assumptions used in the estimate. Understanding the estimation process allows you to tailor the assumptions to your particular situation and arrive at a better estimate of how much money the Freedom approach to requirements could save *your* organization.

Development Cost Savings Estimate

Table B.1 estimates the development cost savings for Freedom's approach to requirements. The estimate centers around Equation 1, which assumes that total development cost is the sum of the costs of developing requirements, design, code, tests, and documentation. (Note that these are technical costs; management costs are not considered because Freedom is a technical rather than a management methodology.) The estimate then makes the following additional assumptions.

Assumption 2

The cost of developing requirements comprises 15 percent of the total development cost. The 15 percent figure is from Berry, who in turn

Table B.1   Freedom Development Cost Savings Estimate

Development cost equation:
  Equation 1: TDC = RC + DC + CC + TC + FDC

Apportionment among process steps:†‡
  Equation 2: RC = TDC * 0.15
  Equation 3: TC + FDC = TDC * 0.5

Substituting 2 and 3 into 1:
  Equation 1a: TDC = (TDC * 0.15) + DC + CC + (TDC * 0.5)

Requirements reuse work reduction assumptions:
  Equation 4: RC_F = RC * 0.5
  Equation 5: $(TC + FDC)_F$ = (TC + FDC) * 0.5
  Equation 6: DC_F = 0
  Equation 7: CC_F = 0

Substituting 4-7 into 1a:
  Equation 1b: TDC_F = (TDC * 0.07) + 0 + 0 + (TDC * 0.25)

Solving equation 1b:
  Equation 1b: TDC_F = TDC * 0.32
or
  Equation 1c: TDC_F = TDC – (TDC * 0.68)

Terms:
  CC = cost of developing the code.
  CC_F = cost of developing the code when all requirements are reused.
  DC = cost of developing the design.
  DC_F = cost of developing the design when all requirements are reused.
  FDC = cost of developing formal documentation.
  RC = cost of developing requirements.
  RC_F = cost of developing requirements when all requirements are reused.
  TC = cost of developing and running tests.
  TDC = total development cost.
  TDC_F = total development cost when all requirements are reused.
  $(TC+FDC)_F$ = cost of testing + documentation when all requirements reused.

† Berry, D.M. 2002. Formal methods: The very idea, some thoughts about why they work when they work. *Science of Computer Programming* 42: 1 (January), Figure 2. http://se. uwaterloo.ca/~dberry/FTP_SITE/reprints.journals.conferences/formal.methods.very. idea.extabst.pdf; http://64.233.167.104/search?q=cache:pb0JleuZlk4J:se.uwaterloo.ca/~ dberry/FTP_SITE/reprints.journals.conferences/formal.methods.very.idea.extabst.pdf+ berry+%22formal+methods+the+very+idea%22&hl=en.

‡ Huang, C. et al. 2004. Optimal allocation of testing—Resource considering cost, reliability, and testing-effort. Department of Computer Science, National Tsing Hua University, Hsinchu, Taiwan; Department of Information Management, Lan Yang Institute of Technology, I-Land, Taiwan; Department of Electrical Engineering, National Taiwan University, Taipei, Taiwan; Computer Science & Engineering Department, The Chinese University of Hong Kong, Shatin, Hong Kong. http://www.cse.cuhk.edu.hk/~lyu/paper_ pdf/PRDC_2004_v2.pdf; http://64.233.167.104/search?q=cache:y5I4ZsEit3AJ:www.cse. cuhk.edu.hk/~lyu/paper_pdf/PRDC_2004_v2.pdf++%22software+testing+cost%22&hl=en.

references requirements cost-effectiveness studies performed by NASA using traditional requirements approaches.

Assumption 3

The cost of developing and running tests, and developing formal documentation, comprises 50 percent of the total development cost. The 50 percent figure is from Huang, and is generally consistent with the author's experience in creating fully tested and documented software for market.

Assumption 4

The cost of requirements development can be cut 50 percent with 100 percent[1] requirements reuse.

Why does 100 percent requirements reuse not cut the cost of requirements development by 100 percent? Because reusable requirements components do not eliminate all requirements work. For example, reusable requirements components are identified via the functionality tree, so the FT must still be created. Also, the external interface prototype must still be developed and evaluated by the users. Although prototype development work is greatly reduced by reusable requirements components, user evaluation remains unaffected. The major savings of requirements reuse, in addition to prototype development, is avoidance of behavior table creation. Together, behavior tables and prototype development comprise the bulk of the effort in the Freedom requirements process. The requirements process effort reduction due to 100 percent requirements reuse, although not 100 percent, is likely to be considerably greater than 50 percent, so assuming a 50 percent cost reduction should be conservative.

Assumption 5

The cost of testing and formal documentation can be cut 50 percent with 100 percent requirements reuse.

The logic here is similar to Assumption 4; that is, many, but not all, test and documentation costs will be eliminated by 100 percent requirements reuse. The cost of unit and integration testing, and programmer-level documentation, would be saved. However, requirements conformance testing and creation of a user manual would still need to be done. Again, the work saved should exceed the work remaining, and the 50 percent cost reduction assumption should be conservative in this case as well.

Assumptions 6 and 7

The cost of design and coding can be cut 100 percent with 100 percent[2] requirements reuse.

Here is the most substantial savings of requirements reuse. Per the jellyfish metaphor of Chapter 8, the bulk of a reusable requirements component lies in the design and code "below the surface" of the black box of the encapsulated requirements. In the case of 100 percent requirements reuse, no design or code, that is, no gray- and white box artifacts, need to be developed. The costs of design and coding go to zero. This is similar to current GUI builders, which create GUIs without coding by use of reusable GUI components. However, current GUI builder components are reusable design components, not reusable requirements components. A GUI design component such as a button can display itself, but does not "do anything" when pressed: that is, no response behavior is implemented. A reusable requirements component implements a complete and fully functional stimulus set of requirements, including both stimuli and responses. Thus, building an application from reusable requirements components is similar to using a GUI builder today except that the result is not just a GUI but a complete application including human, external system, and environment external interfaces all fully functional. In both cases, no design or coding is required.

Assumptions 2 through 7 are reflected in Equations 2 through 7 in Table B.1. Substituting Equations 2 to 7 into Equation 1, and reducing results in Equation 1c. Equation 1c states that the Freedom approach to requirements can reduce *total* development cost (not just requirements development cost) by up to 68 percent.

Maintenance Cost Savings Estimate

Table B.2 estimates the maintenance, or post-release, cost savings for Freedom's approach to requirements. Equation 10 says that total maintenance cost is the sum of the costs of fixing bugs and maintaining requirements, where maintaining requirements includes adding, modifying, and deleting capability requirements in response to user requests. The estimate makes the following assumptions.

Assumption 11

Eighty percent of all maintenance effort is requirements related, and 20 percent is bug fixes.

The 80–20 split between requirements changes and bug fixes is documented by multiple sources, including Ferens, and also Berry.

Table B.2   Freedom Maintenance Cost Savings Estimate

Maintenance cost equation:
  Equation 10: TMC = RMC + BFC

Apportionment between requirements changes and bug fixes:†‡
  Equation 11a: RMC = TMC * 0.8
  Equation 11b: BFC = TMC * 0.2

Substituting 11a,b into 10:
  Equation 10a: TMC = (TMC * 0.8) + (TMC * 0.2)

Requirements encapsulation work reduction assumption: §
  Equation 12: RMC_F = RMC * 0.75
  Equation 13: BFC_F = BFC

Substituting 12 and 13 into 10a:
  Equation 10b: TMC_F = (TMC * 0.8) * 0.75 + (TMC * 0.2)

Simplifying 10b:
  Equation 10c: TMC_F = TMC * 0.8
or
  TMC_F = TMC – (TMC * 0.2)

Terms:
  BFC = bug fix cost.
  BFC_F = bug fix cost with requirements encapsulation.
  RMC = requirements maintenance cost.
  RMC_F = requirements maintenance cost with requirements encapsulation.
  TMC = total maintenance cost.
  TMC_F = total maintenance cost with requirements encapsulation.

† Berry, D.M., Formal methods: The very idea, some thoughts about why they work when they work. *Science of Computer Programming*, 42: 1, January 2002, Figure 3.

‡ Ferens, D.V., Brummert, K.L., and Mischler, Jr., P.R. 1999. A comparative study of model content and parameter sensitivity of software support cost models. In *Proceedings of the 1999 Joint ISPA/SCEA Conference*, San Antonio, TX, June, pp. 1274–1291.

§ Zweben, S.H. et al. 1995. The effects of layering and encapsulation on software development cost and quality. *IEEE Transactions* 21: 3 (March), pages 200–208.

Assumption 12

Requirements encapsulation reduces requirements-related maintenance effort by 25 percent compared to methodologies that do not encapsulate requirements.

No studies have been done on the cost and effort savings due to requirements encapsulation, however, Zweben documents the effects of encapsulation of data structures and other design decisions, that is, traditional OO versus non-OO design. Effort reductions of around 25 percent for OO design were noted. The estimate assumes at least the same level of savings are realized by encapsulation of requirements. It is the author's opinion based on using Freedom for many years that the actual savings due to requirements encapsulation are greater than the savings due to encapsulation of design decisions; that is, the 25 percent figure is conservative.

Assumption 13

The cost of bug fixes is unaffected by requirements encapsulation.

Bugs are errors in design or implementation of requirements, not an error in the requirements themselves. Thus, encapsulation of requirements has no effect on bug fix effort. Traditional OO, encapsulation of design decisions and hardware interfaces, reduces effort for bug fixes. The assumption is that traditional OO is already being used, so no additional savings in bug fix effort is realized by use of Freedom.

Assumptions 11 through 13 are reflected in Equations 11 through 13 in Table B.2. Substituting Equations 11 to 13 into Equation 10, and reducing results in Equation 10c, states that the Freedom approach to requirements can reduce total maintenance cost by up to 20 percent.

Life-Cycle Cost Savings Estimate

Table B.3 estimates the total life-cycle cost savings for Freedom's approach to requirements. Equation 20 simply says that total life-cycle cost is the sum of the total costs of development and maintenance. Beyond the previously documented assumptions, this estimate makes one additional assumption.

Assumption 21

Eighty percent of total life cycle cost is maintenance effort and 20 percent is development effort.

The 80–20 split between maintenance and development was documented decades ago and is commonly accepted throughout the industry. Ferens is merely one source for this figure.

Assumption 21 is reflected in Equations 21a and 21b in Table B.3. Substituting the two Equations 21 plus 1b (development savings) and 10c (maintenance savings) into Equation 20 and reducing results in Equation 20d. Equation 20d states that the Freedom approach to requirements can reduce the total cost of software across the full life cycle by as much as 30 percent.

Table B.3   Freedom Life Cycle Cost Savings Estimate

Life-cycle cost equation:
  Equation 20: TLC = TDC + TMC

Previous results:
  Equation 1b: TDC_F = TDC * 0.32
  Equation 10c: TMC_F = TMC * 0.8

Substituting 1b and 10c into 20:
  Equation 20a: TLC_F = (TDC * 0.32) + (TMC * 0.8)

Apportionment between development and maintenance costs:†
  Equation 21a: TDC = TLC * 0.2
  Equation 21b: TMC = TLC * 0.8

Substituting 12a,b into 20a:
  Equation 20b: TLC_F = (TLC * 0.32) * 0.2 + (TLC * 0.8) * 0.8

Simplifying 20b:
  Equation 20c: TLC_F =TLC * 0.064 development cost with full reuse
              + TLC * 0.64 maintenance cost with req encap

  Equation 20d: TLC_F = TLC * 0.704 total cost with req resuse and encap
  Equation 20e: TLC_F = TLC * 0.84 total cost, req encap only (no reuse)

Terms:
  TDC = total development cost.
  TLC = total life-cycle cost.
  TLC_F = total life-cycle cost with requirements encapsulation and full reuse.
  TMC = total maintenance cost.

† Ferens, D.V., Brummert, K.L., and Mischler, Jr, P.R 1999. A comparative study of model content and parameter sensitivity of software support cost models. In *Proceedings of the 1999 Joint ISPA/SCEA Conference*, San Antonio, TX, June, pp. 1274–1291.

This result is both conservative and optimistic. It is conservative because some of the assumptions are conservative, as explained above. It is optimistic because not all future applications will have access to a full spectrum of reusable requirements components to permit 100 percent requirements reuse, as assumed in the development cost savings estimate. If one carries out the math without the effects of requirements reuse, the result is Equation 20e, which gives a total life-cycle cost savings of 16 percent due to requirements encapsulation only.

In summary, application domains that develop comprehensive suites of reusable requirements components should achieve total software cost reductions of 30 percent or more, but all organizations should be able to reduce total software cost by at least 16 percent if they use Freedom.

References

1. Because the goal is to estimate the maximum savings, 100 percent requirements reuse is used. Requirements reuse of 100 percent may be achievable in specialized domains, but certainly not for all applications.
2. Because the goal is to estimate the maximum savings, 100 percent requirements reuse is used. Requirements reuse of 100 percent may be achievable in specialized domains, but certainly not for all applications.

Appendix C

Glossary

The following is an alphabetical listing of the technical terms and abbreviations used throughout this book.

Abstraction: A collection of data that models a real-world concept or thing. See also: Object.

Access program: (SCR) A block of code, such as a subroutine or method, that provides access to encapsulated information. See also: Method.

Active access program: See Stimulus method.

Administerability: The amount of time and effort per stated duration of time that a system administrator must spend maintaining the system on all the platforms for which he or she is responsible. Measured by time to install and configure. Ranked #4 in default list of Quality Requirements.

Behavior table: A tabular notation that serves as a container for recording the total responses for all stimuli of a single stimulus set in a regular and systematic way.

Black box: Those aspects of the software system that are detectable in the external world including stimuli, external responses, and external communication protocols.

BT: Behavior table.

Canonical design architecture: A design architecture applicable to all programs developed using Freedom characterized by a stratification of modules in which requirements encapsulating functionality modules occupy the upper strata and supporting common service modules occupy the lower strata. See also: Functionality module, Common service module.

Capability requirements: Specific capabilities provided by the stimulus–response behavior of the external system interface. Also called "Functionality Requirements."

Class: A separately compilable unit of code that serves as a template for creating objects in an OO programming language such as Java. See also: Module.

Command stimulus: (1) A stimulus that simply requests a response; (2) a short value or string that identifies the type of record in a command-data stream.

Command-data stream: A simple yet effective generic format for an application-specific protocol that is structured as a sequence of records.

Common service modules: Modules that encapsulate software decisions and hardware interfaces in direct or indirect support of functionality modules.

Compile: Automatic translation of a human-readable notation to a machine-executable notation.

Composition: Object-oriented concept that defines a "has-parts" relationship among objects whereby a conceptually larger object is built up from, or contains, conceptually more primitive objects. For example, an airplane is composed of, or "has-parts" of, fuselage, wings, tail, engines.

Computer science: Subdiscipline of software engineering historically dealing with programming and the code aspects of software, including the application of mathematics to programming.

Context diagram: The highest level of a layered process model in which the entire process being modeled is depicted as a single task box interacting with its external users.

D&I: Design and implementation.

Data stimulus: (1) An input value that may be stored internally by the system or used in some calculation or other algorithm; (2) a value datum associated with a command in a command-data stream.

Design: The gray box view of the software system. See also: Gray box.

Design and implementation constraints: Black box internal information that appears in a requirements specification at the insistence of the customer.

Design and implementation guidance: Black box internal information that appears in a requirements specification on the initiative of the developers.

Design and implementation neutrality: A characteristic of black box requirements that permits use of any design and implementation methodology.

Encapsulation: A technique for improving code maintainability that consists of co-locating cohesive information in a single module and accessing that information only via access programs. See also: Information-hiding.

Enterprise model: A layered process model specifying the business or mission domain process to be automated.

Exception response: The reaction to triggering a stimulus at an inappropriate time or, for data stimuli, with inappropriate data values; includes both external and internal response components.

ER: Exception response, or error response.

Execution speed: The ability of a system to respond at speeds in excess of those required to perform its intended functions in the environment specified for its usage. Measured by time per operation. Ranked #6 in default list of Quality Requirements.

External interface architecture: Same as Stimulus set architecture.

External response: A response that is detectable outside the system black box.

Formal method: A mathematics-based or other rigorous and unambiguous notation for specification of software processes at the requirements, design, or implementation level. See also: Programming language.

FS Functionality screen.

FT: Functionality tree.

Full functional mockup: An interface prototype used to obtain customer feedback on all aspects of the requirements except error responses.

Full functional simulation: An interface prototype used to evaluate all required functionality except error responses.

Functionality: The ability of a system to perform its intended function in the environment specified for its usage. Measured by the percentage of capability requirements met. Ranked #1 in default list of Quality Requirements.

Functionality modules: Modules that encapsulate software requirements.

Functionality screen: A sketch or rough depiction of a human user interface.

Functionality tree: A horizontal tree notation for recording a stimulus set architecture. See also: Stimulus set architecture.

Gray box: Those aspects of the software system that lie within the software system black box but outside the black boxes of the individual modules. Includes identification of the modules and their encapsulated information, module relationships, module stimuli and responses, and module stable interface communication protocols.

High-level process chart: In a layered process model, the layer immediately below the context diagram showing the major tasks of the process, and their data and resource interactions with each other and with relevant external entities.

Implementation: The white box view of the software system. See also: White box.

Information-hiding: Encapsulation in which direct external access to the hidden information is restricted via syntactical or manual means.

Inheritance: Object-oriented concept that defines a "kind-of" relationship among objects whereby a child object automatically obtains, or inherits, information and behavior from parent objects. For example, an airplane inherits the properties of, or is a "kind-of," vehicle and flyer.

Interface prototype: A prototype applicable to requirements discovery due to fully or partially implementing the functionality modules.

Internal response: A response that is detectable only within the system black box.

Look and feel: Popular term for ergonomics of the external interface protocol to human users.

L&F: Look and feel.

Maintainability: The amount of time and effort required for a maintainer to effect a specified change to a system. Measured by mean time to upgrade or repair. Ranked #5 in default list of Quality Requirements.

Method: (1) A block of code with a well-defined stable interface that provides access to encapsulated information in an OO programming language such as Java; (2) an operation on an object. See also: Access program.

Mockup: An interface prototype that implements the actual intended look and feel or protocol.

Module: (1) Generic term for a separately compilable unit of code; (2) (SCR) a unit of work for one programmer or pair programming team. See also: Class.

Natural language: Human spoken or written language. Common variants include prose and poetry. See also: Prose.

New stimulus response: A kind of normal response that activates or deactivates a stimulus set, or individual stimuli of a stimulus set; is always an external response.

Normal response: The desired action or operation performed on detection of a stimulus; includes both external and internal response components.

NSR: New stimulus response.

Object: (1) A cohesive collection of information and associated access programs that models a real-world concept or thing; (2) a runtime instance of a class in an OO programming language such as Java. See also: Abstraction.

Object-oriented: Design and implementation methodology composed of the following concepts: Abstraction, Encapsulation, Information-hiding, Classes, Composition, Inheritance, and Polymorphism.

OO: Object-oriented.

PAP: Performance, accuracy, precision.

PAP requirements: Performance, accuracy, and precision requirements. Performance refers to any required timing applicable to a response or part of a response. Accuracy refers to the permissible range of values or the permissible deviation for a quantity. Precision refers to the number of digits of accuracy of a quantity.

Partial functional simulation: A prototype used to evaluate risk or quality of alternative design and implementation solutions.

Passive access program: A method that borrows a thread of control from its caller. See also: Response method.

PDL: Program design language.

Polymorphism: (literally "many forms") Object-oriented concept that defines a "can-be-a" relationship among objects whereby an object can masquerade as another object from which it inherits properties. For example, an airplane can masquerade as, or "can-be-a," vehicle or a flyer. Polymorphism provides strongly typed programming languages the benefits of weak typing without forgoing the benefits of strong typing. See also: Inheritance.

Process: A systematic approach to creation of a product or accomplishment of a task.

Process model: A specification of a process.

Program design language: Stripped-down programming language syntax consisting of structured flow control syntax and comment-style natural language phrases. Also called "structured natural language" or "structured English."

Programming language: A formal method intended for implementation-level specification of software processes. See also: Formal method.

Prose: Grammatically correct natural language, usually organized into sentences and paragraphs. Use of prose in a requirements specification is a sign of an error. See also: Natural language.

Prototype: A restricted functionality application, often intended to be expendable, built for proof-of-concept or evaluation purposes to help reduce development risk. See also: Interface prototype.

Quality requirements: Measurable attributes of the software system as a whole, ranked to reflect their relative importance to the customer. See also: Functionality, Reliability, Usability, Administerability, Maintainability, Execution speed, Memory demand.

Release: A fully implemented software system in which all requirements slated for the release are implemented in final form complete with all supporting common service modules.

Reliability: The probability that a system will perform its intended functions over a stated time interval in the environment specified for its usage. Measured by mean time to recover (MTTR). Ranked #2 in default list of Quality Requirements.

Requirements: The black box view of the software system. See also: Black box.

Requirements architecture: Same as Stimulus set architecture.

Requirements prioritization: A two-step process for assigning a priority classification or release number to stimuli and stimulus sets.

Requirements reverse engineering: The process of determining the functionality tree or behavior tables of an existing application via systematic observation.

Response: A reaction or possible reaction to a stimulus. See also: Normal response, Error response, New stimulus response, Internal response, External response.

Response method: A hidden (e.g., private) passive access program responsible for generating the external response for one stimulus. The actual implementation may consist of two or more interacting methods.

Reusable requirement: A repetitive stimulus set in the same or different functionality tree.

Robust functional simulation: A full functional simulation in which all error responses are also implemented.

Robust vertical functional simulation: A vertical functional simulation in which the error responses for the functionality being evaluated are also implemented.

SCR: Software Cost Reduction. Naval Research Laboratory project, initiated in 1977 and originally led by Dr. David Parnas, that codified and documented information-hiding as an effective means of reducing software maintenance cost.

Service-oriented: (1) (general) Software methodologies and practices that focus on servicing customer or client needs for functionality and quality; (2) (narrow) architectures and methods related to development of Web services applications.

Simulation: An interface prototype that implements a look and feel or protocol different from the intended delivered look and feel or protocol.

Software engineering: Discipline dealing with all aspects of software throughout the entire software life cycle. See also: Computer science.

Source neutral stimulus set: A textual notation for recording a stimulus set independent of its origination point or implementation technology consisting of the name of the stimulus set over a list of the names of its constituent stimuli.

SQL: Structured query language, a standard notation for accessing relational databases.

SS: Stimulus set.

Stable interface: A method invocation protocol that does not change when changes are made to the method algorithm or information encapsulated by the method.

Stimulus: (1) Anything that causes a response; (2) a message or signal detectable by the system black box.

Stimulus method: A method that has its own thread of control. Responsible for stimulus detection in a functionality module. The actual implementation may consist of two or more methods for creating the stimuli, activating and deactivating the stimuli, and dispatching events.

Stimulus set: A collection of stimuli having functional, physical, and temporal cohesion.

Stimulus set architecture: Hierarchical organization of stimulus sets based on the New Stimulus Response (NSR).

Storage demand: The ability of a system to reside in less storage than that required to perform its intended functions in the environment specified for its usage. Measured by bytes of storage used. Ranked #7 in default list of Quality Requirements.

Technique: (1) A specialized human-readable notation for recording specific software engineering information; (2) generic term for a specialized approach to performing a task.

User interface mockup: An interface prototype used to obtain customer feedback on all aspects of the requirements except required behavior. Usually the preferred type of prototype to deliver to the customer for requirements discovery purposes.

User interface simulation: An interface prototype used to quickly obtain customer feedback on the functionality that will be available to users via the human user interface.

UML: Universal Modeling Language. A set of graphical notations, promulgated by Grady Booch, Ivar Jacobson, and James Rumbaugh, for recording software requirements and designs.

Usability: The amount of time and effort required for a user to make a system perform its intended functions. Measured by time to learn and time to perform specific tasks. Ranked #3 in default list of Quality Requirements.

Vertical functional simulation: An interface prototype used to fully evaluate a subset of the required functionality, usually some key aspect of the requirements around which other parts of the application revolve.

Volatile information: Information that has a high probability of change over the life of the program. Three major categories identified by SCR are (1) design decisions such as data structures and algorithms, (2) software interfaces to hardware, and (3) software system external behavior.

White box: Those aspects of the software system that lie within the module black boxes including complete module source code.

XML: Extensible markup language, a standard for semantical tagging of textual data.

Index

Program maintenance, 12
Programmatic interface
    changes to, 205
    example, 82
Programmatic protocols, 65
    changes to specifications, 199
    example, 72
    XML, 69
Project quality requirements, 179
Prose, behavior recording with, 121
Protocols
    effect of changes to, 205
    external, 21
    programmatic, 65
    stimulus changes in, 200, 210
    stimulus-response, 55
Prototyping, 27
    purpose of, 169
    requirements review and, 145
    types of, 171

Q

Quality
    quantifying, 6
    requirements, 43, 135, 179
        prioritizing, 32
    software, 45

R

Rational process, 31
Regression test code, 99
Release, 176
Reliability, 46, 50
Repetition statements, PDL, 127
Repetitive stimulus set, 96, 101, 146
Required response behavior, 111
Requirements
    architecture, 77, 90
    black box boundaries and, 28
    change example, 207
    change process, 199
    clarification of with prototypes, 169
    cost reduction by precise definition of, 5
    definition of, 20
    encapsulation, 2, 6, 16, 19
        canonical design architecture and, 149
        functionality modules, 155
    external responses as information for, 112

identification of commonalties, 33
    priorities, example, 108
    prioritization of, 33, 105
    process, 27, 31
    rapid evaluation of with prototyping, 176
    reusable components, 98
        example, 99
    reuse, 6, 95
        example problem, 101
    review, 145
    specifications for, 1
    types of, 43
Requirements Encapsulation Design Rule, 3, 146. *See also* design rule
Response behavior, 34
    methods, 156
    required, 111
    specifying in behavior tables, 120
Response classification, 114
Response desirability, 113
Response encapsulation method, 202
Response implementation methods, 156
Response methods
    functionality modules, 162
    interfaces to, 164
Response prescriptiveness, 114
Response recording
    languages, 121
    syntax, 122
Response visibility, 112
Responses, 3, 29
    external, 21
    specification of, 33
    types of, 111
Reusable design libraries, 202
Reusable requirements
    example component, 99
    example problem, 101
Reusable software component libraries, 29, 33
Reusable stimulus set, 97, 146
Reuse library, storage of reusable requirements in, 99
Reverse engineering, external interface architecture, 84
Robust functional simulation, 175
Robust vertical functional simulation, 174

S

Secrets. *See* encapsulation
Selection statements, PDL, 126